Alpine Achievement

A Chronicle of the United States Disabled Ski Team

By: Lori J. Batcheller

Cover photo by Jonathan Selkowitz, Selko Photography, Jackson Hole, Wyoming

1stBooks – rev. 2/1/02

DATE DUE

ILL 3/12			

Demco, Inc. 38-293

"Finally, a bo ... ecoming an elite disabled ski r ...

Ewald Zirbis ...
Head Coach, ...

"An importar ... story of disabled skiing and ad ...

Jeff Leich
Executive Di ...

"A pleasure ... piring stories of courage and ... ."

Kathy Kroll, ...

"A valuable ... on the sport of disabled skii ...

Dr. Robert K ...
Senior Me ... Institute for
Rehabilitatio ...

For Diana Golden Brosnihan
1963 – 2001

Acknowledgments

The author would like to thank the many people who contributed to the successful completion of this book. First, I would like to thank Dr. Mike Messner, one of three Team doctors, who nudged me down the slope when he suggested I write a book about the United States Disabled Ski Team. Without his idea, the story of these incredible athletes would remain untold.

I am also grateful to my teacher and mentor at the University of Colorado in Boulder, Jan Whitt. Her positive feedback, constructive criticism, and lessons in the importance of editing, rewriting, and rewriting again, have greatly influenced my writing career.

I extend my gratitude to the many friends who supported me during the process of gathering information, transcribing tapes, and long hours of writing and rewriting. In particular, I would like to thank Bobbi Unger, who provided a space for writing retreats and listened to both my excitement and anxiety as the book unfolded; Richard D. Smith who provided both moral support and valuable feedback; Alex Hendry who kept me calm during the final stages; and Cindy Nault, Roger Simon, Bob Easton and Mary and Dave Moser, who provided safe quiet havens in Colorado to write.

I thank the entire Disabled Ski Team, including the athletes, coaches, managers, and technicians who agreed to be interviewed for the book, and apologize to those whose stories are not adequately told. A combination of time, technical problems, and space limited the amount of information included in the book. I also thank the many former and non-team members who shared their knowledge of disabled skiing including Jeff Leich of the New England Ski Museum, Bob Emerson, Jack Benedick, Bob Maserve, Peter Axelson, and Rick Isom.

I am especially thankful to Donna Devlin-Young and Kelly Graham, writers who gave voice to the thoughts of Picabo Street and Jimmy Heuga.

Finally I would like to thank the many people who helped behind the scenes including Elise Feeley and all the reference librarians at the Northampton Public Library who generously tracked down phone numbers and resources; Carl Burnett who combined his first-hand knowledge of the Team with his excellent copy-editing skills to improve the manuscript; and Robin Johnson and Jan Unger who sifted through the words and punctuation as only an expert proofreader could. And to the dozens of others, whose names are too many to mention, who promptly returned phone calls and e-mails regarding disabled skiing, adaptive ski programs and equipment, I express my heartfelt thanks.

Table of Contents

Preface

There is something magical about skiing that you have to experience to understand. The crisp, cold, mountain air, the white snow and blue sky. Enjoying the outdoors with friends and family. Feeling completely free yet completely in control at the same time. This is a feeling I knew from a very young age. It was the basis of my career for many years. It is also a feeling I thought I had lost forever.

This book chronicles the stories of people who have overcome their physical challenges to become world-class athletes. I have the alternate perspective of being a world-class athlete who was forced to overcome physical challenges. It was the drive and discipline that I developed as a member of the U.S. Ski Team that helped me overcome the challenges I faced when I was diagnosed with multiple sclerosis (MS). Ultimately, I have been able to come full circle and return to the slopes despite the limitations imposed by my disease.

I grew up near Lake Tahoe and started skiing at two years old. In those days being a member of the ski club was the only social activity around. There were no movies, no nightclubs, and no bowling alleys. There was only skiing. For me skiing was a way of life—the blue sky, the fresh air, and the mountains, a way to enjoy being with family and friends.

In 1949, a new ski area opened—Squaw Valley. The instructors were led by Emile Allais, the man who swept the gold in the 1937 World Championships then went on to coach the French, Canadian, and American national teams. Allais understood that if ski racing isn't fun, it isn't anything.

I remember vividly one time Allais asked me to come skiing with him. I was only seven, and it was a great honor to ski with such a legend. He led me down the groomed trails, with me right on his heels. Then he took me into the trees and the deep powder. In my efforts to keep up I managed to wrap myself around a tree, much to Allais' amusement. I can still hear him laughing as I struggled to free myself. He always pursued skiing for the sheer enjoyment of it, and that has stayed with me since.

I began skiing competitively at age five – slalom, giant slalom, and downhill. I was winning right at the start. At fifteen I was the youngest man named to the U.S. Ski Team. I competed at the 1964 Olympics in Innsbruck, Austria where Billy Kidd and I were privileged to be the first American men to win Olympic medals for skiing when we finished second and third in the slalom. (Billy beat me by a heartbeat). In 1967 I finished third in point standing in World Cup giant slalom and am still the only American to win the prestigious Arlberg-Kandahar race in Garmisch, Germany.

My symptoms also started in the spring of 1967. Before the last race of the season at Alpine Meadows, California I was going up the course, memorizing the gates, and my left eye was getting blurry. Later that year, in Austria, I was taking a bath after skiing and when I got out of the tub my legs were numb. I thought I had frozen my feet. They stayed like that for three months.

I competed in the 1968 Olympics then joined the professional racing circuit, but my symptoms continued. I had vision problems, numbness, and spasticity. My reactions were off and I knew it. I was 23. I'd never been 23 before and I thought these things just happen at that age. Three years later, a neurologist gave me a few simple tests and said, "You have multiple sclerosis." I wasn't very impressed. The neurologist seemed to feel a little sorry for me, but the morning before I had run five miles in 25 minutes. I was in good shape and I thought I was indestructible.

I was advised to avoid any physical or emotional stress that might aggravate my condition. When I told physicians I was getting out of shape, they would say, "Of course you are! You've got MS."

After six sedentary years, I hit what would be my lowest point. But it was also a major turning point. I was divorced, living in Connecticut in a single-room cottage by myself. I felt lousy, I felt dragged down, and it became apparent to me I could no longer do the things my friends were doing—playing touch football and water skiing—and I realized I had been sliding physically. I had lost the ability to run and I was feeling sorry for myself.

I was thumbing through a magazine and came across a quote from Blaise Pascal, who said, "One of man's greatest obstacles is to sit quietly in his room." There I was in that room watching life pass me by. That quote said to me, "You know, Heuga, this is the rest of your life. Are you going to sit here and feel sorry for yourself or get your butt out the door and get back into it?" I realized my greatest obstacle was not MS, but my mind.

I knew I could no longer run, but I thought maybe I could ride my bike. So I grabbed it from where it had been leaning against the wall. I got on it and started to ride and immediately fell over. I got back up and tried again and made it a bit further this time before falling. I kept falling and getting back up until I was completely exhausted. That first time was miserable, but when I got home and thought about it I realized that for those 45 minutes I had actually taken control of my life. I wasn't feeling sorry for myself, I was doing something.

The doctors had told me that exercise could speed up my condition so I was faced with the decision of whether to take the chance of making my condition worse by exercising, while I knew that by exercising I could improve the quality of my life. It was really a philosophical issue. It seemed to me that the days of my life are a lot more important than marking time. I said I am going to exercise because it makes me feel good emotionally. Since it made me feel good, it affected the quality of my life.

What I had done was draw a distinction between my health and my chronic condition. I was angry with the medical community that said to go home and wait for the magical cure—as if there's a cure for life. It was enough for me to be told there was no known cure for MS. That's fine. I just stuck the MS on the shelf and went about improving my life.

When I founded The Heuga Center in 1984, my goal was to help other people with MS make that distinction between having a chronic condition and being healthy. We follow a "can do" philosophy, teaching people with MS how to make the most of their abilities within the constraints of their condition. Exercise, nutrition, and motivation can all help improve a person's overall quality of life. Although it was a radical concept at the beginning, medicine now accepts exercise for people with MS as essential for improving their health, not only as a therapeutic ritual, but also as an overall basis for everyday wellness.

The "beast" is not the physical effects of MS or of any physically disabling condition. It's the uncertainty, the loss of self-esteem and self-confidence that can come with it. When people arrive at The Heuga Center's CAN DO Program they are swept up with all the negative aspects of their lives; when they leave, they're excited about their potential. And nothing has changed except their perception. When people with disabilities begin skiing, they are also often caught up in the challenges of their condition. But gaining a sense of mastery over their body on the slopes gives them a new sense of freedom and helps shift their perception in all areas of their lives.

We've all been dealt the cards, and each of us has the potential to play out a winning or a losing hand. Individuals, even individuals with MS, paraplegia, amputation, or vision impairment, can impact the quality of their lives. What everyone must do is accept where they are and who they are and play the hand they were dealt to the best of their ability. I can think of no other group of people that better embodies this philosophy than the dedicated athletes profiled in these pages.

Being brought up with sports gave me an appreciation for my health, competition taught me the discipline to maintain it, and exercise has been my anchor through the uncertainties of MS. I set goals to give me a sense of control of my life.

Sports for the physically challenged are primarily an anchor to help get some control over our lives. Giving up racing wasn't hard—my life was brought up in skiing, not ski racing. But I missed the feeling of freedom and control of being on the slopes. Thanks to the advancements in adaptive ski technology which are discussed in the following pages, after not being able to ski for several years, I have recently returned to the slopes using a bi-ski.

I still get a wonderful feeling being out in the snow, the cold, the blue sky, and the fresh air. I get as much pleasure from skiing now as I ever did racing. One day last winter I had been out skiing with my family when my oldest son, Wilder, snuggled up to me in my bi-ski and said, "Dad, I never thought I'd get to do this with you again." I think that moment is as precious to me as the memory of any world cup victory.

While the successes of the U.S. Disabled Ski Team are tremendous, I think the greatest victory is that it exists at all. These athletes have demonstrated extraordinary courage and determination in overcoming the challenges that life has presented. To my mind they are winners simply by not allowing their challenges to limit their opportunities. And while I am sure they cherish every race and every medal, I am certain that they, like me, also pursue the sport of skiing for the sheer enjoyment of it.

–*Jimmy Heuga, Edwards, Colorado, September 2001*

Foreword

In February of 2002, approximately 4,000 athletes, 10,000 volunteers, and millions of spectators will flock to Salt Lake City, Utah for the Olympics. Huddled in the cold, they will line up several deep along the steep and icy downhill run that clings to the side of Snowbasin ski area, snaking its way to the valley floor below. The crowds will bear witness to the best in the world hurtling down the hill at speeds exceeding 65 miles per hour, chasing after Olympic gold.

Roughly two weeks after the Olympic torch is extinguished, 1,100 athletes, several thousand volunteers, and close to 150,000 spectators will once again converge upon Salt Lake City. The torch will be re-lit, and skiers who are the best in the world will once again hurtle themselves down the steep and icy Snowbasin runs at speeds exceeding 65 miles an hour, chasing after gold.

Only this time, the skiers careening down the rock-hard gullies and blind knolls of the Wildflower Downhill will be missing a limb. Or they'll be blind. Or paralyzed from the chest down and strapped into a thirty-five-pound mono-ski bucket that doesn't detach in a fall—leaving the skier crashing to earth at full speed with the pulverizing weight of their rig bearing down upon them.

In the winter of 2002 Salt Lake will play host to *two* U.S. Olympic Committee-sanctioned Olympics. It is to this *other* Olympics—the Paralympics—and its athletes that I now pay homage. I write in tribute to their awesome athletic prowess, dedication, skill, and toughness.

"Awe-inspiring" is a term that has often been used to describe the feats accomplished by those of us who ski race on an international level. But it is a term that has never seemed to fit with the reality of my life. However, when I imagine going down those very same courses, at the very same speeds, without the use of my legs, it is only then that I see a scenario truly worthy of awe.

There is nothing heroic about being an athlete. Most of us are born with a gift that we are lucky enough to have recognized and supported by our parents, reinforced and fostered by coaches, and allowed to flourish with the financial and emotional backing of charitable organizations, governments, communities, and corporations. There is nothing remotely mythic about my life and its accomplishments. I see it as akin to building a house or doing well in school or baking a cake: I make a goal and then set about taking the steps necessary to attain it. No mystery. No awe.

Perhaps no other athletes in the world have the label "heroic" or "inspiring" attached to them more than those who are disabled. And while I believe that they are some of the most amazing athletes because of what they have to overcome in order to carve a perfect turn at high speed around a race gate, I also believe that their being viewed through the veil of "inspiration" separates and ultimately stigmatizes them. I have had my mobility impaired and have gone through the long, slow, and painful process of rehabilitation after a serious injury. Yet, when I returned to the slopes and won gold after having been through that, *not once* was the word "inspirational" said about *me*.

It is not "inspirational" to be a ski racer, whether you are physically challenged or not. It is a lot of hard work, pain, devotion, dedication, joy, and attention to detail. Having learned in a small way what it is to have your mobility impaired, I know how much hard work and mental preparation went into recovering from broken bones and severed ligaments. It gave me a small glimpse into the exceptional amount of hard work, determination, and emotional courage behind every world-class disabled skier's journey to the U.S. Disabled Ski Team. So if not "inspirational," how best to describe this journey from loss of limb and mobility to world-class ski racer?

I have seen that the journey involves many things, not the least of which is the fact that one is first forced to be an innovator, pioneer, engineer, mechanic, and test pilot all rolled into one—merely to be able to get equipment that allows one to access the slopes. Then throw in all of the conditioning, training, and preparation that come with the territory of being a National Team athlete. Then there are the financial worries and burdens, which are greater for disabled skiers because they get less funding than the members of other U.S. Ski Teams.

For all of these reasons, I believe that Paralympic skiers are better athletes than the rest of us. Not "heroes" to be placed on an untouchable pedestal or "martyrs" to be mythologized and pitied, but tremendously dedicated and persevering athletes. And there is nothing "inspiring" about it. They have to train twice as hard as the rest of us to compensate for their physical impairments. While I merely put on ski boots and click into my bindings, they are challenged to be both athlete and supreme technician as they work to find equipment that adapts to their disability and allows them to be on snow in the first place. While the rest of us on the U.S. Ski Team just go out and ski, the Disabled Team is constantly faced with overcoming their equipment challenges and evolving their technique around equipment advances in order to carve World Cup turns.

Then there is the stigma that separates them from the world—their "specialness." The mantle of "role model" is one that I wear proudly, but there is a certain amount of pressure that goes along with it. It is pressure I invited into my life when I chose to align myself with media outlets and corporations that would require my becoming a public figure. It is a role that I *chose*, and could walk away from if I wanted to. Having a good friend who is on the U.S. Disabled Ski Team, I know that to be a disabled athlete is to have that role imposed on you by almost every person who sees you. It is as if by the very fact of your disability you now have sprouted wings and wear a halo. All Paralympic athletes carry the burden of implied heroism with a grace and humor that I find humbling. Many athletes who are not disabled have the choice to be just that—athletes. We go out, we do our thing, and we go home to a private lifestyle. Disabled athletes are not given that choice. They must be reminded on a daily basis that they are "special" and "different" and somehow, "other" than the rest of us. That they can ski at all in the face of all that public perception (and, sometimes, misconception) is amazing to me.

I have been given a lot of credit over the past few years for "putting a face" on ski racing and helping to carve out corporate and media niches for snow athletes. But, in closing out this foreword, I want to celebrate a woman who made these advances possible. Like an alpine version of Christopher Columbus, she re-charted the map and re-wrote the rules for making sure that the media and corporations paid attention to ski racing in the United States. Diana Golden Brosnihan, who just recently succumbed to cancer at the age of 38, laid the foundation for much of what I have been credited with when I was still a little kid running around my hometown. Long before the public and media's creation of "Picabo Street," there was Diana Golden.

In the 1980's, Diana skied with a ferocity, power, and skill that captured the imagination of everyone who saw her, and mocked the fact that she had only one leg. She fought for acceptance of disabled athletes and was key to the formation of the U.S. Disabled Ski Team. Diana brought corporate sponsors and media attention to the team. Her tenacious spirit, business savvy and belief in herself as an athlete elbowed their way to the table of international ski racing and made the U.S. Ski Association and U.S. Olympic Committee recognize our physically challenged brethren.

After her death from the cancer which took her leg at age 12 and then waged war within her for most of her life, the New York Times ran a half-page obituary with a picture of her lunging around a gate. In it, she is quoted as saying that she had little patience for the role of someone who accomplished much "despite" her disabilities, and rejected the notion that there was anything inherently heroic about her athletic prowess because she was an amputee. "Athletes don't want to be heroes," she said, "we just want to be good."

In closing, I hope that as you read about the members of the U.S. Disabled Ski Team, you will remember Diana's words. These are real people who, when presented with obstacles, overcame them. They are not heroes, but they *are* some of the finest athletes in the world. In this, they are better than "good." They are supreme. The U.S. Disabled Ski Team is the winningest national amateur athletic team in U.S. history. They have won three times more gold medals alone than the total number of medals *ever won* by able-bodied U.S. skiers in all of the Olympic Games *combined*. I am honored to share hill space, a national team, and the public eye with them.

–Picabo Street, Park City, Utah, September 2001

Chapter 1
A History of Disabled Skiing

Throughout its history, two forces shaped the sport of disabled skiing. Wars and the resulting rehabilitation programs were the catalysts to develop the sport, and accidental injury added to the growing number of people with disabilities who could benefit physically and socially from the sport.

Disabled skiing can be traced to Europe around the time of World War II when wounded German and Austrian mountain troops wanted to quickly get back to what they had been doing—skiing. Attempts were first made to use underarm crutches for skiing in Switzerland, but these efforts were eventually given up. Then, in 1942, Franz Wendel of Berchtesgadener, Germany successfully created a pair of crutches and attached them to short skis, enabling him to maneuver on the ski slopes. Wendel, whose leg was amputated in 1941 from a war injury, entered competitions for the handicapped and by 1943 was being recognized for his "three-track" skiing.

The sport of handicapped skiing soon spread by word of mouth to Austria and, through trial and error, attempts were made to refine the crutch skills. An Austrian by the name of Sepp "Peppi" Zwicknagel, whose disability was caused by a hand grenade during World War II, further promoted the sport of amputee skiing. In 1942, both his legs were amputated, but since he had been a skier and mountain climber before the war, he relearned to ski after overcoming frustrations and ill-fitting equipment. Peppi went on to become a certified ski instructor at the famous Kitzbühel ski school in Austria, where he persuaded the Austrian Ski Association to finance a division for the handicapped. In 1947, the Association organized demonstrations by more than a hundred amputees at the annual races in Badgastein. Dr. Ludwig Guttman, a neurosurgeon, was also instrumental in establishing races in Austria for three-trackers.

Around the same time, both Europeans and Americans began developing rehabilitation programs at army hospitals to encourage amputees to become involved with skiing. The first American skier known to play a role in handicapped skiing was Gretchen Fraser. Gretchen was a rehabilitation volunteer at two U.S. Army Hospitals during the war. Between 1944 and 1945, she used skiing as a rehabilitation technique for

1

amputees. In 1948 she became the first American skier to win a gold medal in the Olympics. Before returning home, she stopped in St. Anton, Austria and donated one of her trophies, requesting it be used exclusively for the handicapped racing circuit.

Several Austrians also helped advance amputee skiing techniques. A ski instructor named Toni Praxmair, owner of the famous Café Praxmair in Kitzbühel, developed and refined instructional techniques by skiing with one leg bound behind him and taught a number of amputees to ski using his methods. Bruno Wintersteller, a member of the Austrian Ski Team who lost a leg in a skiing accident, further developed Praxmair's technique. Wintersteller became an extremely proficient amputee skier and climbed the Matterhorn on one leg many times. Herman Altman, who started a ski school for amputees during the late 1950's in Salzburg, made the techniques more accessible by writing them down in a manual.

Adaptive skiing spread to the United States by word of mouth among amputees, instructors, and specialists in prosthetics. Magazine articles and films about amputee skiing began to appear, prompting more amputees to take up the sport, often by making their own outriggers based on the pictures. Eventually, outriggers obtained from an Austrian firm made their way around the country and were copied and refined. A spirit of openness and sharing, which permeates the sport even today, helped new amputees begin skiing and further develop and refine equipment and skills. National and international amputee races began to appear, offering skiers an opportunity to take the sport beyond the recreational level and become competitive.

In 1952 or 1953 American Bob Engelien, who lost a leg in the Korean War, observed amputees skiing in the Garmisch-Partenkirchen region of Germany. Although he had never skied before, Bob immediately arranged for two days of lessons, which convinced him that skiing would be extremely valuable to other recuperating amputees. He resigned from the military to start an amputee ski program in the United States which became known as the American Amputee Ski School based in Snow Summit, California. Engelien died of cancer a year after his program began, but Scobee Smith carried on his work.

In 1953, Jim Winthurs, a World War II veteran of the Tenth Mountain Division and an avid skier, helped advance adaptive skiing at Donner Summit in California. Although Jim survived combat with his limbs intact, when he became a certified professional ski instructor and ski school director, he worked tirelessly to adapt ski techniques and equipment to meet the needs of disabled skiers. Eventually, Jim became known as the grandfather of adaptive skiing in the United States.

By 1958, on the East Coast, two World War II veterans, Paul Leimkuehler and Stanley Zakas, who were inspired by watching movies of amputee skiers, took up adaptive skiing at Holiday Valley, New York after developing their own outriggers. Since they both had the same foot size and were missing opposite legs, they purchased one pair of ski boots and one pair of skis and divided the equipment between them.

As skiing began to flourish throughout the United States, the sport became especially popular in Oregon, where Dick Martin became the first amputee ski instructor certified by the United States Ski Association, Northwestern Division at the end of the 1962-63 season. Martin, along with Lee Perry of the Portland Junior Chamber of Commerce Ski School, formed the J.C. Amputee Ski School, graduating several classes of students. Hal Schroeder, one of the school's early students, followed in Martin's footsteps and became one of the first certified amputee ski instructors.

Several students from the Portland J.C. group along with other amputees formed the Flying Outriggers ski club, further promoting the sport. In 1965, they wrote and published an instructional manual titled *Amputee Ski Techniques*. Other amputee ski schools began to flourish across America, and by 1962, Kirk Bauer, Doug Pringle and other disabled and able-bodied California skiers developed the National Amputee Skier's Association. As wounded Vietnam veterans, both Kirk and Doug had been students of Jim Winthurs' program. In 1972, the organization became known as the National Inconvenienced Sportsman's Association and included other leisure sports like swimming, sailing, golf, river rafting, trampoline, and water skiing. Their motto, "If I can Do This, I Can Do Anything," reflects their feeling that once they have learned a sport like skiing and feel free to take solo skiing trips, they are no longer handicapped—only inconvenienced. The organization, which changed its name to National Handicapped Sports and eventually to Disabled Sports USA (DS/USA), has active chapters throughout the United States which promote this philosophy and help to make disabled people aware of the leisure activities available to them.

The Vietnam War provided a boost to the development of three-track skiing in the United States when many Americans returned home missing one or more limbs. Beyond the need for physical rehabilitation, doctors recognized the need for a psychological boost and social contact. Skiing, which combines physical strength, flexibility, balance, and endurance with a sense of accomplishment, speed, and an opportunity to socialize with other disabled and able-bodied skiers, provided an excellent rehabilitation opportunity. In the winter of 1968 - 1969, Shepard's ski school began at Arapahoe Basin in the Rocky Mountains west of Denver. The school was a cooperative effort between Denver's Children's Hospital and Fitzsimmons Army Hospital. The Chiefs of the Orthopedics Departments got together and fashioned a program using information they obtained from the German and Austrian programs. The first year, 18 children aged eight to seventeen teamed up with 20 amputee servicemen and learned to ski using gear donated by ski equipment companies and local citizens. Ed Luks, along with his wife, who originally ran the program, later moved to Aspen, then Snowmass, where he established a large adaptive ski school. During the 1970 - 1971 ski season, Winter Park expressed an interest in handicap skiing and the program moved to this resort. Under the direction of Hal O'Leary, the program later become the largest adaptive ski program in the world and now accommodates students representing 45 different disabilities. Hal went on to write the definitive manual of teaching adaptive skiing, *Bold Tracks.*

In the late 1960's and early 1970's, disabled skiing was mainly a recreational sport. The majority of skiers were those who could ski on one ski with two outriggers and those who skied on two skis such as upper extremity amputees. Below-the-knee single and bilateral amputees learned to ski through able-bodied programs using specially designed prosthetic legs and regular ski poles.

Skiing for the blind originated in Norway in 1961, and in 1969 blind skier Jean Eymore began a skiing program in Aspen, Colorado which would become the prototype for blind skiing programs around the country. After losing his sight to diabetes, Jean, who was a senior ski instructor at Aspen Highlands, taught himself to ski again. He and a group of instructors experimented with various teaching and guiding techniques until they developed a system that allowed Jean to navigate the mountain successfully. Convinced their system would work for others, they hosted a week of skiing for seven blind teenagers from the Colorado School for the Deaf and Blind in Colorado Springs and were soon teaching the techniques to instructors from other ski areas in Colorado. Their Blind

Outdoor Leisure Development program, BOLD, spread through word-of-mouth and media coverage and, within a few years, local programs sprang up around the country.

During this same period, another form of disabled skiing known as sit skiing developed to enable other disabled persons, such as paraplegics, to participate in the sport. The European pulk, a sled that cross-country skiers pulled behind them to carry gear, was converted into a kayak-like sled to accommodate those without the use of their legs or those with poor balance. The result was the Aurora, developed by Peter Axelson, a former design engineer. Using two very short ski poles, sit-skiers could maneuver themselves down the mountain. By the winter of 1982, a more functional ski for this population called the mono-ski was invented by mounting a seat on a single ski. This adaptation allowed more maneuverability on the slopes.

U.S. disabled skiing eventually evolved into a competitive sport, reflected in the development of the Handicap Nationals, which began at Winter Park in 1972. Winter Park continued to host this event until the competitions began moving around the country on a yearly basis in 1983. In 1974, the U.S. Handicapped Ski Team was organized and competed in the first international competition, the World Disabled Alpine Championships, held in France. At that time, the main criteria for being on the team were some ability to ski and pay one's own way to the races. From 1974 to 1980, participation by the United States in national events was minimal due to a lack of organization at the domestic and international levels.

Beginning in 1980, the Team started to take a more organized approach, developing selection criteria and organizing itself according to the rules that govern elite sports. The team hired coaches, developed training programs, and began the ascent toward becoming elite athletes. A regional race circuit was developed around the country where prospective athletes could race to qualify to compete in the Nationals and a new level of elite sports was born.

The U.S. Team competed in its first Winter Paralympic Games in Geilo, Norway in 1980. That same year, the International Olympic Committee ratified the Paralympic Games, which had begun in 1976 with Summer Games competitions in Sweden. In 1982 the U.S. Team competed in the World Disabled Alpine Championships. They won their first international medal in 1982—a sign that U.S. disabled skiing was now competitive with the traditional ski powers of Austria, Germany, and Switzerland.

During the 1984 Winter Paralympic Games held in Innsbruck, Austria, the U.S. Team tied with Austria, Germany and Switzerland for alpine medals won. 1984 became a significant year for disabled skiing when the 1984 Winter Olympics in Sarajevo included disabled skiing as a demonstration sport. Three U.S. racers participated in this event, and all three won medals.

As the disabled team evolved, the U.S. Ski Association (USSA)—the able-bodied sport's national governing body—began to take notice, and in 1986 the U.S. Handicapped Ski Team moved from the National Handicapped Sports' jurisdiction to become part of the U.S. Ski Team. This action by the USSA became the model both domestically and internally for integration of elite disabled sports into the associated "able-bodied" federation. The Handicapped Team became officially licensed and logoed as the U.S. Disabled Ski Team (USDST).

In 1986, the U.S. Team competed in the World Disabled Alpine Championships in Salen, Sweden and won 59 medals—almost twice as many as second place Germany. At the 1988 Winter Paralympic Games the USDST retained its number one world ranking as 400 athletes from 22 countries competed in Innsbruck, Austria. That same year, disabled skiing was an exhibition sport in the Winter Olympic Games in Calgary.

In 1998 the USDST took a further step in its evolution as an elite sport when the International Ski Federation (called FIS for the French name, Federation Internationale de Ski) accepted the Disabled Alpine World Cup Circuit and established a disabled sub-committee under the FIS Alpine Committee. Between 19 and 22 nations now compete on the FIS international circuit, which is run like the able-bodied ski circuit. Being recognized by FIS and developing a World Cup series was a further step in building the credibility of competitive disabled skiing.

The current goal of the USDST is to compete as much like the able-bodied version of the sport as possible. Disabled ski racers now abide by the FIS and USSA rules with only a few modifications, most of which are administrative rather than technical. During the 2000-01 ski season, disabled athletes skied in four separate World Cup sites, two in Europe and two in North America.

Opportunities now exist to learn adaptive skiing in dozens of programs around the country. Disabled skiers can choose between both recreational and competitive opportunities, including ski camps designed to develop racing skills. Once equipped with basic skills, many disabled skiers are free to ski at their own comfort level at any ski area around the globe.

Chapter 2
Evolution of Adaptive Equipment

Today's continually evolving adaptive equipment allows disabled skiers to achieve athletic performance equal to, if not exceeding, that of an able-bodied athlete. No matter what a person's disability—paralysis, deformity, amputation, dystonia, or vision impairment—adaptive equipment is most likely available to enable participation in skiing. That means anyone can experience the thrill, excitement, sense of freedom, and psychological boost that come from swooshing down a mountain slope. Freed from the usual constraints that all too often differentiate the disabled from the able-bodied population, on the ski slopes, people with disabilities can participate on equal ground. Skiing is perhaps the perfect sport, for it allows people of all abilities to take pleasure in a common activity side-by-side.

When it comes to adaptive equipment, five categories of skiers exist: three-trackers, four-trackers, two-trackers, sit-down skiers, and vision-impaired. Three-trackers use one ski and two outriggers, which are forearm crutches with 15 to 20-inch ski tips attached to the bottom for three points of contact. The outriggers provide stability and assistance with turning. Typically a three-tracker is someone who has only one functioning leg as a result of congenital deformity, amputation, polio, or other conditions. Four-trackers rely on two skis and two outriggers, allowing them to equalize weight on both legs. A four-tracker has partial impairment in the legs and sometimes also the arms, caused by dystonia, congenital deformity, cerebral palsy, multiple sclerosis, spina bifida, muscular dystrophy, incomplete paraplegia, or double amputation. The four-tracker has the ability to balance in a standing position with the assistance of outriggers. Two-trackers use two skis and ski with or without ski poles. This category includes below-the-knee amputees skiing with a prosthesis, people with dystonia, upper limb amputees, those with upper limb congenital malformations, and those who have suffered a stroke or head trauma. Sit-down skiers include those with paraplegia, quadriplegia, bi-lateral amputation, and weakness or dystonia affecting the legs and often trunk muscles. They ski from a seated position in either a sit-, mono-, bi-, or dual- ski using two short outriggers. Vision impaired athletes require another skier who serves as a guide and a brightly-colored bib, jacket or vest to notify other skiers of their decreased vision.

When adaptive skiing first began, the first outriggers were invented to provide the extra stability and assistance with turning that amputee war veterans required. The first outriggers appeared in Europe in the late 1940's but were crude and heavy compared to today's lightweight models. The early models were made from forearm crutches with tips cut from discarded skis. Jim Winthurs, a ski instructor who served in Italy as a member of the 10th Mountain Division during World War II, brought outriggers to the United States in the early 1950's. Outriggers remained the equipment of choice until the early 1960's when a balance cage was designed to provide more stability. This precarious four-cornered tubular frame with skis on four corners provided balance and allowed those with post-polio syndrome and spina bifida to ski, but was mostly discarded in favor of outriggers, or two-track skiing with or without standard poles. Modern lighter-weight versions of the ski cage called the Slider and Ski Walker are available today and are used to give those with weakness an opportunity to strengthen their legs and improve their balance before advancing to two-, three-, or four-track skiing.

Over the years, several people experimented with improving the heavy 2-to-4 pound outriggers. Ed Luks of Fitzsimmons Hospital in Denver came up with the idea of building a plunger-type device that could be locked into place and would stick out below the ski tip surface to allow walking on the flats or climbing. The plunger could be retracted again for skiing. In the 1970's, some skiers began to experiment with designing lighter-weight carbon fiber outriggers and reducing their overall size and bulkiness. Bob Emerson, a former member of the U.S. Disabled Ski Team, built a custom model that is used today by most USDST three-trackers. These more durable outriggers, constructed of aircraft aluminum, function the same as others on the market, but are lighter weight and more simplistic in design. When these outriggers were tested against standard outriggers in the Olympic wind tunnel, they were shown to produce a lower co-efficient of drag. That means less resistance and faster skiing.

One of the most significant developments for three-track skiers was the patented Flip-Ski. Developed by Ed Paul of Excelsior, Minnesota in the early 1980's, the Flip-Ski can be easily changed from a skiing outrigger into a crutch for walking or climbing. A hand-operated lanyard connects the handle to a spring-loaded mechanism that locks the ski in either position as desired. Today, a similar design made by a Colorado company called Superlite remains the equipment of choice for many beginning skiers, three-trackers, and most mono-skiers. Stand-up skiers who do not need crutches now use a model with no flip-up mechanism. Most racers who use outriggers—three-trackers, four-trackers, and mono-skiers—prefer a competition model which has no brake on the back of the ski and which flips down rather than up when the lanyard is pulled, allowing for quicker starts in a racecourse.

While above-the-knee amputees generally choose to ski as three-trackers without their prosthesis, many below-the-knee amputees wear their prosthesis, putting them in the category of two-trackers. When adaptive skiing began, below-the-knee amputees used a suspension system composed of a waist belt, joint, and corset. Side stays, generally made of metal, ran up the outside of the leg and attached permanently to the prosthesis. The corset portion, generally formed out of leather, went around the thigh and was laced up along the front, much like a shoe. The corset bore some of the weight, adding control, and stability to the knee, and also helped distribute weight evenly. The whole prosthesis was suspended from a belt that fit around the skier's waist and usually attached to the joint and corset.

Today, some seasoned skiers and ski racers still use a form of joint and corset to help distribute weight and stabilize the knee, but advances in materials and levels of expertise in designing and fitting prosthesis have brought new levels of comfort, durability, and stability. Today's prostheses and suspension components are made from a variety of composites, plastics, and gels. Plastic models that last longer and don't stretch unnaturally are replacing leather corsets, which tend to stretch out when an athlete is sweating. While older prostheses were built with fiberglass, newer ones are made of carbon fibers that provide a lightweight, streamlined, ultra-strong leg. Lightweight and resilient braces allow skiers to flex forward in their ski boots, shifting their weight forward on the ski and allowing them to more closely imitate the movements of able-bodied skiers. The latest brace technology can also stabilize a skier's anatomical or "real" knee to provide extra support. Multi-axial knee hinges now imitate the movements of the anatomical knee and provide enhanced strength and rigidity on either side of the joint.

In addition to changes in materials and design of suspension systems, the basic design of leg prostheses has also changed. Typically, the older systems were exoskeletal in nature, with a hard outer shell and soft interior. Today's prosthesis more closely matches a person's natural leg design, using an endoskeletal system with a soft foam cover. The hard structure of the prosthetic leg is internal, like a skeleton. To improve comfort, gel systems and similar liners buffer external forces, decrease shear forces, and provide better shock absorption. In addition to providing cushioning, the interface material improves the contact between the amputee's skin and the prosthesis. This not only prevents skin breakdown but also improves the skier's ability to feel the ski's contact with the snow. Adding a neoprene or latex suspension sleeve—an elastic device designed to slide over and cling to both the prosthesis and the skier's thigh—both enhances the fit of the prosthesis and helps to accommodate the additional weight and leverage that result from adding a ski to the prosthetic limb.

Even with all the adjustments and adaptations mentioned above, skiers who use a walking prosthesis for sports may still not feel properly aligned or may have the feeling they might come out of the prosthesis while skiing. Today, many amputee athletes prefer to wear a custom-designed sports leg when skiing. The sports prosthesis fits into a regular ski boot and is fitted for each individual athlete to avoid problems with canting, wedges, or uneven weight distribution. Besides being custom-fit, sports prostheses differ from walking models in the amount of flexion. The built-in bend places the skier in an athletic stance and maintains a good, straight alignment. Athletes can also choose from ankle components with or without motion.

In addition to using outriggers and a prosthesis when appropriate, stand-up skiers may also employ wedges, lifts, and cants to equalize their weight and increase forward lean. Wedges, made of dense foam, compact cardboard, or wood, can be placed inside the ski boot to help accommodate any lack of flexion in the skier's ankle or prosthetic limb. Generally, ski boots are built with a forward lean to keep the skier's ankle flexed, so adding a wedge inside the heel section of the ski boot naturally angles the prosthesis forward as it rests inside the boot. Placing a lift under the opposite boot makes up for the shortening of the skier's body that may be caused by this alteration. Wedges can also be used under the heel of the boot to increase forward lean and place the skier in a more athletic balanced stance.

Cants, which come in various thicknesses, are basically plastic wedges placed to the inside or outside edge of the ski boot to help ensure flat contact between the ski and the snow when running on flat terrain. This is especially important for an amputee skiing with a prosthesis because they do not have fine motor control down at the foot to keep a ski running flat.

Today almost all ski racers ski on lifts, which reduce vibration and distribute the forces out over the ski. With the new "shaped skis" that have become common in the past five years, which allow the skier to create such sharp angled turns that the boot can hit the snow while the skier is on edge, lifts serve to keep the boot off the snow. For safety reasons, FIS regulates the height of lifts. For adults, the distance between the base of the ski and the top of the boot sole could be no greater than 55 mm for the 2001 - 2002 season. This rule applies to all standing disabled skiers.

Upper-limb amputees, who fall into the category of two-track skiers, often choose to ski without a prosthesis using one or no poles. Bi-lateral arm amputees must overcome the challenge of moving their weight from side to side without the use of arms, which can be done by practicing balance activities on and off the slopes. Otherwise, these skiers do not need special adaptations other than some assistance transporting equipment, getting into their ski gear, and when using some ski lifts.

In the late 1970's, a new form of adaptive equipment that allowed wheelchair users to ski appeared in America. The first version of the sit-ski, named the Smith Sled after its designer, was a variation of the pulk, a toboggan-like ski from Europe. Smith added long aluminum runners to the bottom of the kayak-like sled so that the sit-ski would run a track in the snow. The Smith Sled could be tethered down the slope by an able-bodied skier or skied independently by leaning side to side and dragging shorted ski poles in the snow.

In 1978, Peter Axelson created another form of the sit-ski as a student project at Stanford University, which was later funded by the Department of Veterans Affairs Rehabilitation Research and Development Center. The Arroya sit-ski opened up new skiing possibilities to paraplegics, quadriplegics, and others unable to ski standing up. Peter, a product design major who became a paraplegic in a rock climbing accident when he was nineteen, came up with the Arroya design after trying the Norwegian pulk at Winter Park Ski Resort. According to Peter the pulk was fun, but skiing it felt like "going down the hill on a lunch tray." Peter used his design background and knowledge of skiing and water skiing to come up with a more controllable sit-down ski. Like a water ski, the Arroya had a concave bottom surface, with the addition of four inward-facing stainless-steel edges. The curved design provided more stability to the ski, and the tunnel underneath the ski created by the steel edges allowed more control and maneuverability. Because of the design, a skier could more easily turn the ski by shifting his or her body weight forward and stop the turn by leaning backwards and dragging short ski poles. With the Arroya, an experienced sit-skier could easily traverse, turn and stop on both beginning and intermediate trails. For beginning skiers and those with more severe impairments, the Arroya could also be guided down the hill by an able-bodied skier using a tether.

While the Arroya was an improvement over the Smith Sled, many skiers still found it difficult to turn when using one shortened pole to pivot on the uphill side and the other to grab the snow and pull on the downhill side. Sit-down skier Rick Isom decided to improve upon the shortened ski pole by replacing the basket with a large metal washer. The new design carved through the snow and served as a perfect pivot. Later Rick added metal arm braces that came up both sides of a skier's arms and attached with Velcro. This addition shifted torque away from the wrist.

Peter decided to release the Arroya design, and later other concepts developed by his company, Beneficial Designs, into the public domain so that none of the designs could be patented. This generous decision allowed anyone to use the design to build his or her own version of a sit-ski, and soon other skis based on the Arroya model appeared on the market, making skiing possible for just about anyone with a physical disability.

While sit-skis did get a broader range of people with disabilities on the mountain, including paraplegics, quadriplegics, bi-lateral amputees, and others with poor balance or leg weakness, the equipment has its limitations. Inexperienced skiers, who often drag their arm along with the pole, may end up with dislocated shoulders and elbows. The sit-ski is also relatively heavy, requires two people to lift onto chair lifts, and provides limited turning ability for those who want to advance to higher levels of skiing. Despite its limitations, several models of sit-skis are still used today at many adaptive ski programs for beginning and more severely impaired skiers, and those who prefer to ski sitting close to the ground.

Also during the 1970's, another type of sit-down ski was developed by some double-amputee Austrians. This ski consisted of a tractor-type seat with a spring beneath it, attached to a normal ski. While this model allowed double-amputees more maneuverability on the slopes, it was not designed for use by anyone with legs. The ski gained minimal exposure in

Europe, and throughout the 1970's and early 1980's sit-skis remained the only option for disabled people with legs.

By the mid-1980's a new piece of equipment called the mono-ski began appearing on European ski slopes. The first popular mono-ski was designed and patented in Germany by a father whose son was disabled and used a wheelchair. Called the GFL Technik, this sit-down ski was designed from fiberglass automobile parts. The GFL featured a stiff kayak-like shell that fully enclosed the skier's legs and lower trunk and attached to a ski via a frame and suspension system. This less-rigid ski allowed the skier to turn more easily by leaning from side to side and using shortened outriggers for stability and turning ease.

The real advancements in sit-down skiing, both in the United States and abroad, began when Andre Deville, Director of the Swiss Paraplegic Association, arranged two international workshops for disabled skiers to share adaptive ski technology and equipment. In both 1985 and 1987, the Association brought together people from over 13 different countries for the event. Peter Axelson, along with a dozen other U.S. sit-down skiers including Rick Isom and Kirk Parkhurst, attended the first event where they saw the GFL, brought it back to the United States, and began making improvements on the design. Instead of a fully enclosed shell, a bucket-type seat was developed with a foot rest and knee straps to hold the legs in place. The U.S. models also used a pivot seat suspension mechanism that allowed the ski to articulate under the seat while keeping the feet stationary in relation to the ski. Kirk, who became the first certified mono-ski instructor in the United States, added a pin to release the leaf spring suspension, allowing the shell to be lifted up onto chair lifts while the ski and leaf spring stayed underneath. Although considered an improvement, the design was a bit problematic for getting off the lift because the leaf spring often got caught under the chair. Peter improved upon the idea by adding a latch, allowing the skier to lift up the seat and lock it in place. This became the first self-loading mono-ski, paving the way for sit-down skiers to be completely independent. If ice and snow developed on the mechanism, however, another person was required to stand on the back of the ski while the skier lifted up the seat and locked it. The following year, Peter added a shock absorber and arrived at the 1986 World Championships in Salen, Sweden as the only skier with a complete shock absorber on his equipment. With his single-pivot mono-ski, Peter won the downhill race by four one-hundredths of a second.

Rick then added one more feature to the mono-ski design to solve the problem of ice formation and make mono-skiers truly independent. By redesigning the lever arm and shock absorber system, as the skier extends the leverage arm and pulls in an arc backwards, the shock absorber pivots down and forward causing the body of the ski device to raise up into a locked position. This position is then high enough for the chair lift to come under the ski device. With outriggers flipped up, the skier can easily move into the loading zone and get on the lift independently. At the top of the lift, the ramp automatically pushes the skier up, allowing him or her to easily push off the seat. By shifting the lever forward, the mono-ski seat is lowered and the skier is ready to ascend the slopes. This design is now used all over the world.

By the 1988 World Championships held at Mutters ski area in Austria, the whole league of mono-ski equipment had accelerated and every skier showed up with shock absorbers. Both Peter and teammate Rick medalled at the Championships and were the only sit-down skiers to receive their awards from a wheelchair—the other skiers were able to walk with prostheses or other assistive devices.

Improved seating, or bucket design, was the other major contribution Americans made to the original mono-ski. While general bucket designs allow just about anyone to ski in a mono-ski by adding foam or clothing to fill in the spaces around a person's body, they don't offer the stability needed by many paraplegics—especially those with higher level injuries. When Peter learned about orthotics heating in which a seat could be molded to an individual's body, he incorporated the idea into a custom-made mono-ski. He and Alan Siekman, a seating designer at Children's Hospital at Stanford, made the first orthotic full-seating system using a molded plastic polyethylene shell. The long process involves taking a large piece of hot plastic and wrapping it around a person's buttocks to come up with a custom-fitted shell. While the seats fit well, the procedure takes four people to shape the plastic and costs more than the mono-ski itself. The orthotic seats also tend to crack and break because of the changing temperatures, trunk bending and body forces exerted on them when skiing. Because of this, Peter, like other ski designers, later chose to use a carbon-graphite shell that is less flexible but more durable.

Peter's single-pivot mono-ski eventually sold under the brand name of Shadow, which while very simplistic in design compared to newer models, is still preferred by a few mono-skiers, most notably Sarah Will.

Other versions of the mono-ski, all based on the GFL but with improved features to provide more comfort, control, and independence to sit-down skiers, were also appearing on the market. Dan Fallon, an American whose wife was partially paralyzed from an accident, decided to purchase the GFL patent after he saw how much his wife enjoyed learning to mono-ski under Kirk's instruction. Dan later developed his own version of the mono-ski, known as the Yetti, and eventually sold his company to Mike and Genie Goodman, a couple whose son Joel has spina bifida and skis in a mono-ski. The Goodman family, including their other son Jeff, runs what is now known as RadVentures. The Yetti features the single-swing-arm suspension developed by Peter, and combines Kevlar, the substance used to make bulletproof vests, with fiberglass to create a tough outer seat shell. Inside the shell the skier uses a molded foam seat that fits the skier perfectly, adding more comfort and control.

While the single-pivot design allowed Peter to win races, he still wasn't completely satisfied since his feet tended to bounce when he hit bumps. Following the 1986 World Championships, Peter decided to make one more change to his mono-ski based on a concept already used by teammate Rick. To resolve the comfort issue, Rick had designed a fully suspended mono-ski version using a four-bar parallelogram, having four equal-length supports. Peter designed his version with a four-bar linkage, with two pairs of bars of differing lengths. With this design, as the body rises up and down while skiing, every part of the body stays level.

The final advancement to mono-ski design was a standard binding release system developed by Europeans to attach the ski to the mono-ski. This metal or plastic plate, called a "boot" or "ski foot" and featured on many of the latest mono-skis, clicks into a regular ski binding. This allows ski racers to easily change between a training ski and a freshly waxed and sharpened racing ski right at the race start. The boot also allows for minor adjustments in placement to accommodate individual athletes.

One of the challenges with mono-skis has always been correct placement of the mono-ski frame on the ski. Companies used to mount the seat halfway between the ski's tip and tail. This placement could sometimes put the mono-skiers three inches forward of the optimal position resulting in more falls because, without enough pressure, the tails of the skis lifted off the snow at high speeds. Equipment manufacturers now mount the binding device at "boot center," the optimal position for most skiers. This change makes it possible for the mono-skiers to successfully finish their turns.

While advancements were being made in the mono-ski design, another type of sit-down ski began to appear on the ski slopes. Called the bi-ski, this design features two skis and two steering levers, providing more stability than the mono-ski but more maneuverability than a sit-ski. Rick was one of the first bi-ski designers. His bi-ski has mechanically articulating skis with long parallelogram arms and a bucket that rests very high off the snow. In addition to providing more stability, bi-skis also have a more protective frame that goes around a skier's entire body. While good for general recreation, the heavy bi-ski is more difficult to maneuver through the tight turns of a racecourse. Later, Paul Speight, a Denver-based adaptive ski manufacturer, designed a bi-ski that is very low to the ground, providing more stability. Like mono-skis, bi-skis now come in a variety of models including those with and without shock absorbers, assisted-load models, and self-loading styles with hydraulic pumps. While some skiers begin in a bi-ski for the added stability then advance to a mono-ski as their balance and ski technique improve, others choose to remain in the bi-ski.

The latest sit-down ski to enter the market is known as a dual-ski, which is a hybrid between the mono-ski and bi-ski. With dual-skis, the bucket is very close to the snow and works well for disabled people who need assistance to ski down the hill. A handle bar added to the back of the ski allows an able-bodied person to easily turn the ski right or left. As with other sit-down skiers, the dual-skiers can learn to turn themselves using outriggers for stability. Fixed outriggers can also be attached to dual-skis for those unable to hold outriggers, but since these fixed outriggers have the disadvantage of occasionally pushing a skier downhill on steeper slopes, the use of a tether is always recommended.

Following the 1997 U.S. Extreme Snowboarding Championships in Crested Butte, Colorado, another adaptive skiing device entered the market. Then ex-USDST member Chris Devlin-Young had been invited as the first mono-skier ever to fore run the event. When snowboarders approached Chris saying they had friends who were in wheelchairs and had no way of returning to the sport they loved, Chris decided to pursue the idea of developing a mono-snowboard. Over the next several months, he developed some prototypes, and in February of 1998 tested them out on some experienced snowboarders. The result was the Trench Digger 5000 (TD5000) – the first mono-snowboard.

The TD5000 features a base plate that allows the mono-ski rig to easily attach to the bindings of any snowboard. Because of its wide base, getting on and off a chair lift is simplified. The TD5000 is also easier to transfer into from a wheelchair than a narrow mono-ski.

As a ski instructor and Head Coach of the New England Disabled Ski Team at Loon Mountain, Chris quickly saw the possibilities of using the TD5000 as a teaching tool for mono-skiing. Because of the snowboard's greater width, and thus greater stability, adaptive skiers could more quickly achieve balance and gain self-confidence on the hill. Chris developed an accelerated mono-ski learning method by first putting adaptive skiers on the TD5000, then progressing them to a mono-ski once they learned the basic turning techniques. His first student, a T-5 paraplegic who snowboarded prior to his injury, quickly gained his sense of balance the first day. He fell only once during the four-day learning period—unlike mono-skiers who generally fall many times while learning—and progressed to the mono-ski by the fourth day. When the TD5000 was demonstrated at a Stratton Mountain clinic in Vermont in April of 2000, participants immediately recognized the accelerated teaching virtues for beginning skiers.

While the final class of disabled skiers—those with vision impairments—do not require the use of highly specialized adaptive equipment, extra precautions must be taken to ensure safety on the mountain. When blind skiing was developed in the 1960's, the only piece of adaptive "equipment" required was a brightly colored ski bib or jacket, available now most often in fluorescent orange, printed with the words "Blind," "Guide," or "Visually-impaired." The only other adaptation for blind skiers is an able-bodied guide who skis in front to direct the vision-impaired skier safely down the mountain. The presence of the guide is often enough assistance for a mildly vision-impaired skier, while those with more impairment, or complete blindness, require the addition of hand and/or voice signals to inform them of where to turn and changes in terrain. The guide and skier work closely as a team and learn to adjust signals according to the snow and weather conditions.

All the advancements to adaptive equipment over the years have contributed to making disabled skiing what it is today—both a widespread recreational venue and an elite competitive sport. Whether a person is severely physically disabled and requires complete assistance down a hill by an able-bodied skier, skis recreationally on his or her own, or chooses to race, everyone can now enjoy being outdoors with his or her friends and family on the ski slopes.

Chapter 3
Medical Classification and Scoring

Opportunities now abound for disabled skiers to enjoy racing, testing their abilities first at local recreational NASTAR courses and then progressing through a system of increasingly competitive races nationwide. The ultimate achievement in disabled racing today is to make one's national team and compete in the Paralympic Games, where physically disabled athletes from around the world represent their countries in elite international competition. But even those who choose only to compete locally can experience the challenge and thrill of racing against the clock and gaining mastery of their bodies through skiing slalom gates.

Most ski areas across the country offer NASTAR courses, a fun and easy way for ski racing enthusiasts of all ages and abilities to compete against one another in the largest recreational ski race program in the world. Participating resorts set up an open giant slalom racecourse and a season-long race schedule, where entrants compete against a time determined each year by a member of the U.S. Ski Team (Picabo Street for the 2000 to 2001 ski season). After each race, skiers are given a handicap expressed as a percentage of the pre-determined race time. Disabled racers also receive a handicap discount based on the NASTAR Pacesetting Trials skied by members of the USDST. Participants can win gold, silver, or bronze medals based on how well they fare for their age and gender category. By continuing to participate, racers also receive a resort, state, and national ranking which can be viewed at the NASTAR web site. Physically challenged categories exist for upper extremity impairments, blind, two-track, three-track, four-track skiers, and mono-skiers.

Disabled skiers may also begin racing through events sponsored by Disabled Sports USA (DS/USA), a national organization established in 1967 by disabled Vietnam veterans. In addition to sponsoring two levels of races across the country, DS/USA also offers development camps where skiers can learn to race, and racing camps where they learn more advanced technical skills.

DS/USA-sponsored level 1 races are held on USSA-sanctioned NASTAR-type courses and offer the beginning ski racer an opportunity to taste racing. According to former Team member Paul DiBello, who now heads the race training program at the National Sports Center for the Disabled (NSCD) at Winter Park, the format of level 1 races is to keep things simple and just have a good time. The idea is to expose disabled skiers to ski racing to see if they like it. If they do, opportunities exist to move on to higher level races. During the 2000 - 2001 ski season, DS/USA sponsored twelve level 1 races, and plans to expand the program to at least twenty races a year.

Level 2 races allow skiers to qualify for the U.S. Disabled Alpine Championships, commonly referred to as the Nationals, that include four racing events—slalom, giant slalom (GS), super G, and downhill. USDST members often compete in level 2 races closest to their hometowns, giving new racers an opportunity to see where they stand against the top ski racers and to be seen by Team coaches. One of the level 2 races is the Ski Spectacular which takes place each December in Breckenridge, Colorado. Most of the USDST members are usually in attendance for a few days before the Ski Spectacular, which provides a great chance for up-and-coming racers to meet, train with, and get coaching from the Team. Other well-attended level 2 races include the Huntsman Cup in Park City, Utah, the Eastern Regional in Waterville Valley, New Hampshire, and the Columbia Crest Cup in Winter Park, Colorado, organized by the NSCD, which takes place just prior to the Nationals.

The USDST coaches assign different racers to different races based on skill level and disability class. While an A Team standing skier may be entered into able-bodied races instead of many level 2 races, a C Team mono-skier may compete in most or all of them. In addition to participation in level 2 races, members of the USDST compete in a busy international-level race schedule. Usually in January, the Team travels to Europe for the opening World Cup races of the season then returns for World Cup events in the United States and Canada in February or March. World Championships take place every four years in February or March, and the Paralympic Games take place every four years in March two years after the World Championships. The Paralympic Games immediately follow the able-bodied Olympics and are held in the same city, although race venues are not always the same. For example, while the alpine skiing events at the 2002 Olympics in Salt Lake City will be held at three different ski areas, the Paralympic events will all be held at one resort—Snowbasin. The final racing event of the year, the U.S. Nationals, generally takes place during late March and is usually held at a Western resort, although it occasionally takes place in the East, as in 2000 when it was held at Mt. Snow, Vermont. The Team's winter schedule concludes with a fundraising event in Vail in early April put on by the Cable and Telecommunications Industry.

While racers enjoy competing in all competitions, the Paralympics, World Championships, and World Cup are considered the most important events, drawing the best competitors from around the globe. Although the World Championships can be even more competitive because of stricter qualification standards, the Paralympics are considered the premier event, partly because of the large crowds of spectators they attract. In fact, the Paralympics are the second largest sporting event in the world, second only to the Olympic Games. At the Nagano Paralympics in 1998, 151,376 spectators, including the Emperor of Japan, showed up to watch 571 racers from 32 countries compete. The 2002 Paralympics in Salt Lake City expect to draw up to 1,100 athletes from 35 countries for events which include cross-country skiing, biathlon, and ice sledge hockey, in addition to alpine skiing.

When many different disabilities began becoming involved in ski racing, a classification system was established to ensure that each athlete compete only against competitors with similar disabilities. For members of the USDST, a factor system, similar to a golf handicap, was later developed to reduce the number of different race classes competing and thereby increase competitiveness. Additionally, the USSA able-bodied point system is used to determine racer's starting position.

Any athlete who wants to compete in disabled races from the level 2 race series up must undergo a medical classification exam prior to racing to determine his or her disability classification within one of three more general categories: sit-down, stand-up, and blind. Stand-up and sit-down athletes are examined by a doctor, assisted by a physical therapist. Before their first international event, racers are examined by classifiers from the International Paralympic Committee, the governing body for World Cup and Paralympic skiing. These classifiers are generally a physician or other medical professional. Vision-impaired athletes are examined by an ophthalmologist assisted by a consultant ophthalmologist.

Stand-up skiers are generally the easiest to classify since many are arm or leg amputees. From the information obtained during the examination, stand-up skiers are placed into one of seven categories, LW1 to LW9, depending upon their disability. (See Appendix F for a complete description of each class.) Classifying an amputee usually takes little time, as B/K amputee Mary Riddell explains. She basically took her prosthetic leg off during the examination and they classified her as an LW4. Stand-up skiers with muscular weakness undergo a strength evaluation, and stand-ups whose deficits are complex and not easily classified, such as George Sansonetis who has dystonia, are placed in the LW9 class, informally known as the "trash class."

Sit-down skiers include skiers who lack the balance or strength to ski in the stand-up category, including paraplegics and bilateral amputees. Bilateral amputees are classified as LW12/2s. Because paraplegics often do not have a complete spinal cord injury, and thus have partial use of muscles below the level of injury, a more involved examination is performed to classify them into three levels, LW10, LW11, and LW12/1. This examination is based on their exact disability, level of injury, strength, and balance and includes medical documentation of the disability, six functional tests, and observation of the athlete in practice or competition. Once a racer's disability-related history has been documented, the evaluation team tests the athlete's hand, arm and shoulder strength, flexibility, coordination, and range of motion. The athlete then sits on a testing board composed of a carpeted wooden board with three stabilizing straps, mounted on two semi-circles. The athlete's ability to lean forward, backward, and side-to-side on this tilt board is tested with their hands behind their head, folded across their chest, and extended out to the side. The final functional test involves the athlete's ability to pick up a ball from the floor, bring it above the head and place in on the floor next to the opposite hip. These motions assess the athlete's trunk balance, coordination, strength, and flexibility, which ultimately affect the ease with which an athlete can maneuver a mono-ski. Observing the athlete in practice or competition assists in classifying borderline cases, disabilities involving coordination deficits, and cases of suspected cheating. Paraplegics often require more than one classification exam, especially if they undergo any surgery to stabilize their spine or remove rods since their level of function may change.

Blind skiers are divided into three groups, B1 to B3, depending upon the severity of their vision loss. This ranges from complete blindness to partially sighted (visual acuity above 20/600 to visual acuity of 60/600 and/or visual field of more than 5 degrees and less than 20 degrees). All classifications are based on the best eye with best correction.

In addition to the internationally-approved medical classification system, the USDST divides its team members into three classes based on performance—A, B, and C. Most athletes begin on the C Team, although on rare occasions an exceptional athlete with prior racing experience is placed on a more advanced team. In 2001, the USDST added a development (D) Team, where athletes can hone their skills before moving up to the C Team.

A well-defined list of criteria determines when athletes move up to the next level. To be named to the C Team, an athlete must place in the top three and ski within 7 percent of the winning factored time at level 2 races and ski within 10 percent of the winning factored time at any international races entered. Besides having good technical skiing skills, racers must also demonstrate the willingness to dedicate the time to training and racing required to be a USDST member. To remain a member of the Team, the athlete must advance to the B or A Team by the end of two seasons.

To move up to the B Team, an athlete must medal in one discipline at the Paralympic Games or World Championships and be within 7 percent of the winning time. They must also medal in 25 percent of all World Cup races entered, and achieve 75 percent podium finishes at USDST-designed selection races in all disciplines. They must also ski within 5 percent of the winning factored time and within 5 percent of an A Team member or within 5 percent of the winning time at international races.

To make the A Team, an athlete must win a gold medal in the Paralympics or World Championships, medal in 50 percent of races entered at the Paralympic or World Championships, and medal in 50 percent of World Cup races entered. Racers must also finish ahead of current A Team members in international and national races, and all aforementioned results must be within 5 percent of the winning time. A Team members are also expected to meet B and C Team criteria.

At all competitions above the NASTAR level, which uses just one course, disabled races include the same four events as able-bodied races— downhill, super G, giant slalom and slalom. These four different disciplines test each skier's technique, balance, strength, and courage. While all events involve skiing through gates, downhill and super G races are considered speed events and giant slalom and slalom are considered technical events, since gates are placed closer together.

The downhill course is designed mostly for speed, grace, and smoothness in turns. Gates are placed the farthest apart, and the course generally goes from the very top to the very bottom of a slope, taking one to two minutes to run. This one-run event includes a variety of challenging turns and gliding sections in which the skiers reach the highest speeds of all the alpine disciplines—up to 65 miles per hour or more. When skiing a downhill course, racers keep a tuck most of the way. In downhill, unlike the other events, skiers are allowed two training runs. Racers take advantage of these to prepare for race day by first inspecting the course then taking the first training run to feel what the course is like. With a day to think about the course and their first run, during the next training run racers tighten up their line a bit and take a few more chances. By the third day, racers generally know exactly what to do. Of course, if snow conditions change between pre-race days, skiers must rely more heavily on course reports from the coaches.

According to blind guide David Marchi, part of the technique in downhill is trying to keep on the ground and just be smooth and aerodynamic. While there are rarely jumps *per se* in disabled downhills, since skiers are racing so fast, it's not uncommon to get air off the little rolls in the hill. But catching air slows skiers down, so they try to keep themselves on the ground.

In super G, gates are placed slightly closer together and the course is a bit shorter. Like downhill, super G is a one-run event of high-speed turns, which may also include gliding sections, but skiers are not allowed any training runs. Because of the closer gates and shorter course, skiers have to work more on their turns, making the race more technical.

Giant slalom, considered a technical event, is about half the length of a super G but has almost twice as many gates. The event is more about turning and being as smooth as possible while carrying speed through the turns all the way down the slope. For each athlete in giant slalom, times from two runs are combined to obtain a total time, which determines the winner.

Slalom is the most technical of the four events, demanding extreme agility and balance. The course is about a quarter the length of a super G, and the whole course can often be seen from one place. With around 70 gates, the event requires very quick turns, and racers often hit or "block" the gates as they go through, allowing them to take the tightest possible line. Two-legged skiers usually block gates with plastic guards on their hands and shins, while three-trackers may also wear chest and shoulder pads that allow them to block the gates with their bodies. In recent years, some mono-skiers have also begun blocking slalom gates, although styles vary widely. As in giant slalom, slalom also combines times from two runs.

In addition to the four disciplines, a combined award for the all-around ability of a racer is sometimes awarded based on the combined times from all the races in a series. To win the overall, a skier must show consistency, finishing each individual race and placing high enough according to a point system to be above everyone else. The overall World Cup title is one of the most coveted prizes in both able-bodied and disabled ski racing.

While all classes of skiers race in all disciplines, not every team member races in each discipline at every event, and because each discipline tests different abilities, racers with differing disabilities find particular races more challenging. Clay Fox, a below-the-knee amputee who skis with a prosthesis and suspension system, finds slalom the most difficult race because of the quickness required. "Your leg tends to slow you down a bit," he says. Left forearm amputee Csilla Kristof also finds slalom the most challenging for two reasons. First, because it's a shorter course where the skiers don't really have a chance to get a lot of speed, pushing off at the starting gate becomes even more important. With only one arm, Csilla and other arm amputees can only push off from one side, losing some power. Arm amputees are also at a disadvantage when it comes to cross blocking—a technique used by skiers when they're turning around a slalom gate. While racers generally usually use their opposite arm to block a gate, i.e. using the right forearm to block a left turn and vice versa, Csilla needs to use the same arm to block on both sides. Blind skiers also find slalom the most challenging, since the gates come up on them so quickly, and the guide must successfully guide them through the tighter turns.

Until the mid-1990's, medals were awarded for each of the 15 classifications, LW1 through 12 and B1 through 3. These days, most races award medals in just three categories of racers: sit-down, stand-up, and blind, employing the same many-class system to determine an athlete's factor. The factors are based on data accumulated over many years that show how fast members of each disability class are—or have been—on a particular course. While not yet a perfect system, the factor system results in awarding fewer medals, which increases the competition and gives more credibility to the medals. The system is also easier for the general population to understand. The Paralympics continue to be run differently from other disabled races. Instead, they are based on the older, multi-class model. Under the International Paralympic Committee system, if enough athletes are present in any one category from around the world to make up a field of 10 racers, no factors are added. If the size of the category is less than 10, two or more classes compete against one another using factors to make a field of 10. Thus, more medals might be given at the Paralympic Games than at the other races, depending upon the numbers of skiers in each classification.

While at first many racers were resistant to the factored scoring system because it meant fewer chances to win, and although the system continues to be refined and perfected, most now see the advantages of a larger race field and fewer awards. Vision-impaired skier Andy Parr, who is often the only vision-impaired athlete at U.S. events, likes the factor system because it means more competition. He does not feel a true sense of accomplishment when receiving a medal unless he's competed against many other racers. And, Andy says, more competition means it will be easier to raise money—an ongoing challenge for Team members—because top results and medals are meaningful to sponsors.

In addition to the disabled race circuit, many USDST members also compete in able-bodied races, thanks to Diana Golden, an amputee ski racer during the 1980's. Because of Diana's athleticism in able-bodied races, where she skied with regular poles rather than outriggers, in 1985 the U.S. Ski Association passed the Golden Rule, reserving places for elite disabled skiers. Competing in able-bodied events gives disabled skiers more opportunities to race and more challenging competition, ultimately making them better racers. Able-bodied ski racers gain the opportunity to see the abilities of their disabled competitors. Racing in able-bodied races also reveals that the USDST is not only the best disabled ski team in the world, but that its members rank among some of the best able-bodied skiers as well. Legendary Above-the-knee (A/K) amputee skier Greg Mannino, who has been with the Team for 16 years, has placed in the top 20 against able-bodied racers at the able-bodied Nationals. And Below-the-knee (B/K) amputee Mary Riddell has her sights set on being one of the best female ski racers in the world, able-bodied or disabled.

Chapter 4
Skiing Blind

Imagine skiing down a racecourse in an international competition at 60 miles per hour unable to see straight ahead because of a dark spot in the center of your field of vision. Or skiing through gates and over rolls while looking through a video camera covered with Vaseline, blurring the entire course. Blind ski racers face challenges like these every time they race down a mountain.

For Maine native Andy Parr, who skis in the B3 class, many variables, including lighting and colors, affect his ability to see his surroundings. Both extremely bright and dark days affect what he can see. And sometimes things just disappear from Andy's sight for no reason, then might come back into focus again. While he can navigate a recreational ski run on his own, he is unable to see gates, making high-speed racing impossible on his own. Instead, he and other blind ski racers rely on trained guides to navigate them safely through a racecourse at high speed without missing a gate or hooking one with a ski tip. Andy's guide, David Marchi, wears a bright yellow jersey which serves as a beacon for Andy to follow.

Because of their limited vision, blind skiers also learn to rely on sensing variations in terrain rather than seeing them. Andy's body tends to automatically shift its weight in a certain way according to certain conditions because of the way he feels the snow. But even with some tactile feedback and a guide's cues, uncertainty is a constant factor in blind ski racing.

Like other vision-impaired racers, Andy has found it more difficult to gain the technical skills required to carve fast turns because he questions what he's seeing. As he races down a course, Andy wonders whether a gate is really a certain distance away or if he's really seeing the right "line" – the path racers take through the gates. Because of this, vision-impaired skiers often ski with a stiff and rigid stance, sliding turns rather than carving them. While many blind skiers do eventually learn to carve turns, it may take them longer than a normally-sighted skier.

While making tight turns in slalom continues to be a challenge, Andy finds downhill races the most nerve-wracking. Knowing the goal in downhill is to race down the mountain as fast as he can, fear is a natural part of ski racing for Andy, as it is for most racers. In fact, in downhill, he says he's scared out of his mind, partly because his experience in downhill is limited. But despite his fear, Andy trains and races downhill because he knows the best way to improve and become a well-rounded racer is to be a good speed skier.

Andy was not always vision-impaired. He grew up as an average kid in Rockland, Maine and started to ski recreationally at Camden Snow Bowl when he was seven. While signs of vision loss began as early as age ten to thirteen, they didn't become apparent until Andy's grades began to suffer in high school. Andy had no way of explaining his poor grades. His teachers thought he was just being lazy and encouraged him to wear his glasses since he had a slight astigmatism. It wasn't until Andy failed the eye examination for joining the Marines between his junior and senior year that his problem was finally diagnosed.

The doctors discovered that Andy has Stargardt's disease, a rare recessive genetic form of macular degeneration that leads to a loss of central vision. While it cannot cause total blindness, Stargardt's can cause legal blindness, and with loss of central vision, seeing straight ahead can be difficult to impossible. Fortunately for Andy, side vision is not greatly affected so despite the progressive central loss, he can walk around, recognize his surroundings, and with the help of low-vision devices, do some limited reading.

Despite his vision impairment, as a senior Andy raced with his high school able-bodied team. Since his vision was 20/200, meaning Andy can see an object from 20 feet away that a normally-sighted person can see from 200 feet, Andy didn't really consider himself disabled. In fact, to look in his eyes, most people wouldn't even notice Andy has an impairment, and at the time, he wasn't aware that ski racing for the blind even existed. Even when he did learn about racing opportunities through a vocational rehab counselor at what was then called the Maine Center for the Blind and Visually Impaired (now the Iris Network), Andy didn't pursue the sport. Andy figured disabled ski racing was only for those with more severe vision deficits. Besides, Andy had his sights set on college and being the type of person who focuses on just one thing at a time, he put other activities out of his mind.

After college, Andy worked at the Sugarloaf/USA ski area as a seasonal employee where he had the opportunity to witness the U.S. able-bodied Ski Team compete in the Nationals. Seeing racers like AJ Kitt, Tommy Moe, and Picabo Street led him to pursue the idea of disabled ski racing. Andy first contacted the U.S. Association for Blind Athletes, who gave him the name of Brian Santos, a former USDST blind skier who won every race at the 1994 Paralympics in Lillehammer. Through a phone call to Brian, Andy felt inspired to see how he'd do in a more competitive race against people with similar disabilities. But another two years passed before Andy actually began racing as a disabled skier with a guide.

As Andy soon learned, finding the right guide can be a challenge because the blind skier and guide must work very closely together, much like a marriage. Both skiers are individuals, but must work as a team. The guide must also be available for all the scheduled training camps and races. It's very difficult to find a guide with "no strings attached." Andy credits his first guide, Erle Morse, with helping him get into racing. But Erle soon found that the busy race schedule kept him away from his family too often. Andy's second guide, a recent college graduate, retired from racing to pursue his career. Andy also discovered the importance of finding a guide who is a good ski racer when his guide missed a gate during a slalom run. Andy followed and was disqualified. Fortunately for Andy, when he made the Disabled Team, Head Coach Ewald Zirbisegger introduced him to David, and the team has been training and racing together ever since.

David was already an experienced guide, having previously skied with former Disabled Team member Bobby McMullen. Bobby, who had vision loss related to diabetes, was a B2 class racer with very little vision in one eye and 20/1000 in the other. But despite his vision loss, Bobby was an incredible skier, or in Andy's words, "He really ripped."

Over several months, Andy and David developed a system of racing that Andy describes as "synchronized skiing." David skis in front wearing a bright yellow top so Andy can see him better, with Andy following close behind. Because Andy has some vision, David uses few voice signals. Instead, he and Andy first inspect the course and memorize the turn combinations. During the race, David calls out the beginning of each combination, adding additional voice signals if there's a rhythm change. To indicate a big roller in giant slalom, super G, or downhill, David will sometimes bring his arms way out to indicate this to Andy. On rare circumstances when the rhythm of a course changes, David yells back to him. But most times that's not necessary. Other than taking note of David's particular body angles and where he's turning, and looking for a few extra signals, Andy's job is to chase David down the hill, trying to ski exactly the same line.

David got involved with skiing when he was four years old and has been skiing ever since. Before becoming a blind guide, he skied competitively, becoming the best ski racer at Mt. Shasta, California. When David's ski coach Ray Watkins, who served as a guide for Brian Santos, asked David if he wanted to be Bobby's guide, David readily took on the responsibility. But after a year, it was obvious Bobby and David's personalities weren't a match, so David returned to school, living first in Durango, then in Breckenridge where he raced and got some coaching experience. In the summer of 2000, Ewald invited David to join the Team as a staff member, and shortly after that Andy arrived without a guide. That's when David took on the role.

With the heavy racing and training schedule, David no longer gets the chance to race on his own, but he doesn't mind. He'd given up his own dreams of making the able-bodied team because of the full-time training that would be required. Instead, David enjoys helping Andy achieve his goals. And while being a guide lacks the glory of winning a medal, David says that's not why he's in the sport. Like other team members, coaches and behind-the-scenes staff, David just truly enjoys being with the people involved in disabled skiing. "They're a great group of guys and girls, amazing athletes. I enjoy being with them because they have such good spirit," he says.

As a guide, David also serves as a coach, helping Andy with mental preparation, which David considers to be 70 percent of winning. When David first takes on the role of guide to a blind skier, his job is to get to know the athlete's level of skiing, how fast he can go, and any unique fears and concerns. But once they're on a course, the skier's abilities take a back seat in David's mind to making sure he's taking them in the right place. When he raced with Bobby, who didn't have much peripheral vision, it was vital David steered clear of other skiers on the mountain because if anything came in Bobby's way, Bobby would either panic and stop, or run into them.

An additional challenge facing David is to ski at the right speed, making sure he doesn't get so far ahead that the blind skier can't see him. If he does, the racer gets intimidated. David occasionally needs to look back to see that the racer is right behind him—an additional challenge when skiing 50 or 60 miles per hour through gates. When skiing with

Bobby, David found that when the space between them got too large, Bobby would tense up and ski badly. When they were tight, Bobby was a lot more comfortable. In fact, while guiding Bobby during a race in Canada, David once skied too fast, and Bobby just pulled off the course. Unlike Andy, Bobby also needed voice signals to get the rhythm of the gates and big hand signals in downhill to indicate rolls.

Like the other disabilities represented in disabled skiing, vision impairment is not the same for every athlete, and comes with its own unique challenges. While the physical challenges amputees and paraplegics face are obvious, vision impaired skiers face many unique challenges when skiing through gates at high speeds. With so many different vision impairments, skiers have many different levels of sight and therefore different needs. And no two guides do things the same way.

Because Andy has some vision, people often don't understand the challenges he faces on the slopes. "People see me walking around completely fine and don't have any idea that I have a vision impairment," he says. That can sometimes be a negative thing for Andy and other blind skiers, whose vision can be affected simply by changes in lighting and by certain colors. People often don't understand that vision impairments are not "black and white." In between blindness and full sight, there are many shades of gray.

Both Andy and David would love to see more blind racers on the American team. Right now Andy's the only visually impaired racer on the Team. In contrast, Spain has 200 blind skiers at its national championships. At World Cup races, Andy gets a lot of competition from athletes from other countries, but in U.S. races, he's the only one skiing in his class.

While Andy loves being a ski racer, he admits it's a lot more work than most people realize. "They think we're just on vacation all the time," Andy says. "We're busting our butts all the time to raise money, to stay fit, to keep up with all the other good disabled skiers around the world. It's not a vacation by any means for us, it's definitely a job."

Chapter 5
Above-the-Knee Amputees

As a veteran member of the USDST, for years, A/K amputee Greg Mannino has been the man to beat. During his 16 year career with the Team, he's seen athletes come and go and has watched the evolution of disabled ski racing from a weekend warrior sport to its current status of elite international competition. Along with the changes in rules and regulations, Greg has witnessed the level of athletics improve. As an LW2, Greg is part of one of the largest classes of disabled skiers in the world. At international races, he competes against as many as 40 amputees, while even on the U.S. Team, he's apt to race against five or more team members vying for the number one spot.

Greg grew up skiing at Big Bear in Southern California where his parents had a cabin, but he claims he actually learned to ski on the streets. He and his friends were never at the ski resort because they could just click into their skis in the front yard and ski down the streets. Always athletic, during high school Greg competed in track and field and made the varsity football team when he was a sophomore. Greg also skied recreationally as much as he could and competed on his school's ski team. But Greg didn't really start skiing competitively until 1982, three years after the accident that would change his life.

While trimming palm trees in California the summer before his senior year in high school, Greg got into some high power lines. Instantly, he felt electricity enter his right hand, race through his body and ground through his feet and steel-toed boots. He describes the experience as being just like the cartoons showing a character being electrocuted. His hair stood on end. He jumped around everywhere as the electricity burned him. After the accident, his leg was so badly burned the doctors were forced to amputate it above the knee.

While he was still in the hospital, Bonnie St. John, an above-the-knee amputee racer who competed during the late 1970's and early 1980's, introduced Greg to disabled skiing. She assured Greg there was still life out there, even as an amputee, and convinced him to give three-track skiing a try. The next April, Greg was back on the slopes. He quickly realized he'd found a sport where he could go fast, have fun chasing his friends down the mountain, and participate alongside his family. Despite his previous racing experience, Greg only skied recreationally for the next three years. With the encouragement of his friends, he eventually turned his focus towards racing.

Greg's first taste of national ski racing was a humbling experience. When he qualified for the national championships, he thought he was going to do really well. Instead, David Jamison and Danny Pufpaff, who were the top LW2 guys at the time, just "smoked him." Rather than becoming discouraged, being badly beaten motivated Greg to train and try to become just as good. After spending a year on the development team improving his racing skills, Greg was named to the USDST in 1986. As Greg climbed through the ranks of disabled racing, he's become the man to beat. As teammate George Sansonetis says, "When it comes to speed, he just blows our doors off."

Around the time Greg was training to make the Team, Monte Meier was growing up in Minnesota. In May of 1979, when Monte was just eight years old, his simple childhood was permanently changed. While outside in the yard of his family's home, Monte got caught up in the garden tiler behind the lawn tractor his father was driving. Monte became a right above-the-knee amputee.

Monte remembers little of the accident, nor of the following days in intensive care where he faded in and out of consciousness. He does remember opening his eyes, seeing the nervous look on his parent's faces and hearing his mom tell him he had one leg. His nonchalant response led his mother to gently shake him and ask, "Did you hear what I said?" "Yes, you said I have one leg," Monte replied, laying back down and giving in to medication-induced sleepiness. When his mother asked what he thought about it, Monte answered with a question. "Well, can I still run?" After a pause during which Monte noticed the hesitancy on his mother's face, she finally replied, "Yes, you can run." With that reassurance, Monte lay back down and fell asleep, knowing he would be able to continue to do whatever he wanted.

That's what Monte's done ever since. As much as possible, he's lived his life like he did before he lost his leg. His parents treated him no differently with one leg than two, and he credits their support for the success he's had both on and off the ski hill.

In the late 1970's, waiting for the swelling in an amputee's stump to go down before fitting it with a prosthesis was standard procedure, so Monte spent the next several months on crutches, attending school and participating in activities with his friends as much as he could.

One day the following fall, when Monte's parents were away at work, a phone call came in from the Courage Center outside Minneapolis. When they explained who they were—an organization that helps children and adults learn to ski—Monte felt excitement well up inside. He and his mom had always wanted to learn to ski. Soon after that, Monte experienced his first taste of skiing, which almost made him change his mind.

Monte's first ride up the mountain on a chair lift with no safety bar high above the ground as he says, "freaked him out." Once he and his instructor were on the snow, things didn't get much better. Skiing was much harder than Monte had expected. Trying to balance on one leg with two outriggers felt strange, and when he and his instructor got to a steep pitch on the bunny hill, Monte encountered man-made snow blasting from snow guns. Since, as Monte says, he was skiing about two miles per hour, he was soon covered in white, and while his instructor skied on ahead, Monte fell and got mired in the sticky, fresh snow. Finally, Monte got himself up. After he'd worked his way to the bottom of the hill, his instructor asked if he was ready to do it again. Monte immediately responded, "Heck no, I want to get out of here. This is just dumb." Fortunately for Monte, his instructor didn't give up that easily and convinced him to do another run. The second run took less than half the time as the first, but still being upset, Monte didn't want to let on that he was actually starting to have fun. By the third run, Monte was successfully navigating himself down the hill and had forgotten everything about the first run. By the end of the day, he was hooked.

For the next two years, Monte spent as many weekends as he could skiing in the Minnesota hills. When he started to get bored with the short easy runs, someone suggested racing. Monte quickly learned racing skills, began to compete in regional races, and qualified for the Nationals in 1986 when he was fourteen. When he went to Jackson Hole for the competition and first saw the USDST in action, he was both humbled and inspired. As he watched Greg Mannino ripping down the hill while just free-skiing, Monte was in awe. Being out in the mountains and watching Greg's unbelievable performance hooked Monte on racing right away. Skiing the Rockies was breathtaking, unthinkable compared to the hills in Minnesota. From then on, Monte knew he had to become a USDST racer.

Throughout high school, Monte mixed ski racing with varsity wrestling. When he graduated, he moved to Winter Park to train full-time for two years, but wasn't selected to the USDST. Disappointed, Monte decided to return to Minnesota and finish school. He ended up training with the Afton Alps Alpine Club, an able-bodied USSA team. While training full-time with the team, Monte also entered disabled races and finally made the USDST B team the following season. Monte credits the training he received from the able-bodied Afton Alps coaches with helping him make the Disabled Team. The coaches were excited and more than willing to work with him.

While Monte doesn't acknowledge any notable differences between the coaching he received through the Winter Park disabled program and at Afton Alps, he feels the experience of racing with able-bodied skiers gave him the extra spark he needed to push him further. Admittedly, he'd become somewhat complacent toward the end of his Winter Park training. With the able-bodied team, he was on unfamiliar ground, and Monte didn't know what to expect from himself any more than the other kids knew what to expect from him. Monte just wanted to show them what he had, and being with them gave him the extra motivation to "kick into a higher gear."

Monte, whom Greg describes as "quite possibly the funniest human being on earth," still credits much of his success both on and off the slopes to his Mom's words in the hospital that he can be anybody he wants to be. While he may look different on the outside, Monte's still the same person he was before he lost his leg.

During the late 1970's as Monte was adjusting to having a disability, Jason Lalla, who was the same age, was growing up in New Hampshire. On a warm summer day when Jason Lalla was eighteen-years-old, he hopped on his motorcycle to ride the familiar eight miles from his home in Lake Sunapee to go for a swim. On the way back, he revved up his bike to see how fast he could go, a habit that had once gotten him up to 140 miles per hour without any disastrous consequences. This time he wasn't so lucky. Just when he reached 100 miles per hour, he crashed.

Instead of spending the summer following high school graduation working a summer job, Jason spent it in the hospital, recovering from the left leg above-the-knee amputation incurred from the accident. After being discharged, Jason was fitted for his first artificial leg at a prosthetic shop in Bedford where he met Bob Emerson, a former USDST member. While Bob fitted Jason for his prosthesis, he and other prosthetists told Jason about disabled skiing. But Jason wanted nothing to do with disabled sports. After all, Jason was a jock. During high school, he'd excelled in both lacrosse and hockey, and hockey had absorbed him completely. Before the accident, Jason could probably have walked on to any Division II college hockey team.

Despite losing his leg, in a sense, Jason didn't consider himself disabled. His picture of disabled athletics wasn't very positive. He pictured people who were either elderly, barely able to get around, severely handicapped, or stumbling around on walkers, more like the Special Olympics. For some reason, Jason didn't picture athletic people being disabled. Like most people who become disabled, Jason didn't know anyone else with a disability, except for Bob at the prosthetic shop. So instead of pursuing sports, Jason just hung out with his friends. But, as Jason would later discover, the picture he had of disabled sports was completely wrong.

One of Jason's high school coaches just happened to be involved with a ski company and he set Jason up with all the necessary equipment to start three-track skiing. Soon after Jason got on the slopes, he fell in love with the sport and began skiing recreationally as many weekends as he could. The more he skied, the better he got, and people began encouraging him to race. But by then, Jason already had his sights set on going to college.

In the fall of 1993 Jason moved west and spent the next two and a half years trying out different majors at the University of Northern Colorado. When he finally realized nothing really appealed to him and decided he was just wasting his money, Jason turned his visions towards ski racing. Little did he know that his ideas about disabled sports would soon shift completely.

Jason moved back in with his parents in New Hampshire and contacted Bob, who told him about an upcoming ski camp being held at nearby Waterville Valley by USDST members and then head-coach Mike Brown. Bob suggested that by attending, Jason could meet Team members and get an idea of what he'd be up against. By that point, Jason felt he was a pretty good skier, but knew nothing about racing. He decided to attend, figuring he would either go out and win, or get his butt kicked. He didn't envision himself anywhere in between. On the last day of camp, Mike invited anyone interested to join the Team in Vail for training. After spending the week with the Team, Jason's mind was already made up. That night he packed, and the next day he moved to Vail.

Jason decided to set what seemed like a realistic goal, giving himself three years to make the Team. He figured that if he didn't get selected by then, he'd go back to school to pursue something else. When he first began racing alongside the Team, Jason surprised himself by placing eighth against the best skiers in his class and by the third year, he was beating some of his mentors.

While Jason's racing skills improved, his attitude towards disabled athletics also completely changed. Being among the disabled ski racers and seeing their zest for life and positive attitudes, Jason realized that none of them felt like they were disabled—and neither was he. During his third year racing, Jason made the Team.

In looking back on his experiences since his injury and his role as a ski racer, Jason feels it's been a good ride. When he was first injured Jason felt like his life was over. Now he realizes that it had only just begun. He doesn't look at being an amputee as a detriment at all. Instead, Jason says his life is better now than it ever was.

While Greg, Monte and Jason's lives changed suddenly from accidents, by his early teens, New York native Dan Kosick began to frequently experience a tingling sensation in his leg and ankle. Figuring the tingling was harmless, Dan ignored it until the symptom became worse during his sophomore year in high school when he became more involved in sports. Unsure what the problem was and thinking the sensation was perhaps caused by tendonitis, Dan's doctor casted the lower leg hoping rest would alleviate the symptoms. When the tingling persisted, Dan saw another doctor, who performed a biopsy. The test revealed a tumor inside Dan's nerve that made his foot unusually sensitive. Whenever Dan hit his ankle, the nerve would react. Although the sensation did extend up Dan's leg, the doctors would have no idea how far the tumor went up unless they did more surgery. Since the biopsy had revealed the tumor was benign, Dan decided to just resume his normal sports schedule. But when the symptoms became worse, Dan took the chance of having the tumor removed, despite the fact that the surgery could cause permanent nerve damage. The surgery revealed that the tumor stemmed from Dan's foot to behind his knee. After two days in the hospital, the doctors informed Dan the tumor was turning cancerous and recommended above-the-knee amputation as the best course of treatment.

Before the operation, Dan tried not to think about how serious his condition could be. At fifteen, his biggest concerns were whether he would still be able to do everything with his friends and whether girls would still want to go out with him. His thoughts revolved around his ability to run, play sports, and keep up his normal daily life. Fortunately for Dan, prior to the surgery, his aunt met an amputee skier in a ski shop and asked if she'd be willing to talk to her nephew. Jean Marie, who happened to be a physical therapist, readily agreed. Before Dan underwent surgery, Jean Marie came to visit and answered all Dan's questions about how to drive with and walk on an artifical leg. She also told him about skiing, and directed him to the best physical therapists and prosthetists in the area. When Dan finally lost his leg, he was surrounded by supportive people, including his new amputee friends. Following the surgery, Dan underwent a six-month course of chemotherapy. During that time, he never once heard anyone say he wouldn't be able to do any of the activities he wanted to try. And, no one ever tried to tell him he would have to be extra careful not to hurt his remaining leg. Instead, his friends and family all offered to help him achieve whatever he wanted to do. By the end of August, Dan was ready to resume an active life.

After learning to run on his prosthesis, Dan resumed his previous position as goalie for the high school lacrosse team. Dan also started swimming again, mostly to get into shape. His lifelong dream of succeeding as a competitive swimmer ended when he lost his leg. With one leg, he felt too self-conscious in his Speedo swimsuit to compete again on the school team. But when his old coach approached him, explaining that the team was weak and needed more good swimmers, Dan joined in and actually became a faster swimmer than before because he was determined to beat the kids with two legs. During his senior year, he even became captain of the team.

Although Dan had skied recreationally with friends a few times a year since he was nine, he had never thought of competing. None of his family members skied, and, after all, skiing was an expensive sport. But when his new amputee friends introduced him to the Sunday adaptive program at nearby Greek Peak, Dan discovered that skiing could become a vehicle for his competitive nature.

His first day back on skis was the coldest day of winter. While Dan was sweating from picking himself up from falls and fighting the ski, his instructor was freezing cold, but never went inside to warm up. Despite the falls, Dan never got frustrated and found himself improving with every run. Since Dan had just turned sixteen the previous summer and gotten his license, he was free to drive himself to the ski hill whenever he chose—which turned out being almost every day during the winter.

Dan quickly found out that skiing was actually more affordable after he lost his leg because of reduced prices for skiers with disabilities and because he needed only one ski at a time, which he got by contacting ski companies directly. As Dan started talking to people involved with skiing, including instructors and coaches, he became a much better skier. When he learned about an upcoming ski camp at Pennsylvania's Jack Frost ski area where coaches from the Winter Park disabled program came every year to find disabled skiers interested in racing, Dan was ready. The Greek Peak program paid his way for the week where he met ski racer Danny Pufpaff and race program director Paul DiBello. And when Dan learned about the USDST and the possibilities of competing and traveling, he set a new goal—to make the Team.

Dan spent the next year attending training camps with Winter Park, including a summer camp in New Zealand, a two-week Christmas camp before the Huntsman Cup, and the Hail Mary Camp—so called because it is the athletes' last prayer to learn how to ski fast—to prepare for Nationals. The following year he moved to Colorado to train full-time. By the summer of 1997, he made the Team.

While people often express their amazement at Dan's leg strength and ability to balance on one ski, he finds it relatively natural. After all, once he lost his leg he needed to acquire that balance and strength just to live everyday life. Like other USDST members, when he's not on the slopes, Dan enjoys other sports. Once in a while he competes on his mountain or road bike, but mostly bikes for cross training. He also heads out to San Diego each year to compete in at least one section of the Cast Iron Man Triathlon, generally the swimming section because he still loves to swim and finds it the easiest leg of the race to prepare for. While Dan skis as a three-tracker, he mountain bikes with a prosthesis and has another leg for lacrosse and jogging. In the future, he plans to do some long distance jogging.

Although many of today's USDST members began skiing at an early age, twenty-nine-year-old amputee Sandy Dukat's appointment to the Team in 2001 following just four years on the slopes proves that with talent, hard work, and perseverance, becoming an elite ski racer is possible even without an early start.

Sandy was born without a femur bone. The rest of her leg, including the tibia and fibula bones along with her entire foot, was fine. Because of the missing bone, Sandy did not have a normal socket or fully developed muscles around her left hip. Since her lower leg and foot would not be functional, at their doctor's advice, her parents decided to have it amputated when she was four. The amputation allowed Sandy to wear a full-length prosthesis as an above-the-knee amputee.

Growing up in Ohio without mountains or big hills, Sandy never gave any thought to skiing. Like many who grow up as the only disabled person in a community, Sandy wasn't aware of disabled sports, but actively participated in able-bodied sports throughout her childhood. As the youngest of four children in a family of natural athletes, chasing her older siblings made Sandy automatically competitive. Only years later, when Sandy moved to Chicago to work as a social worker at the Rehabilitation Institute of Chicago and joined an amputee support group, did she first learn about opportunities in disabled sports.

At one of the meetings, which were mainly composed of men over sixty who had lost a leg to diabetes, the group members asked Sandy why she hadn't swam and participated in other sports for the disabled. Sandy could only reply that she didn't know. The next thing Sandy knew, her support group got her signed up for swimming and she became a member of the U.S. Disabled Swim Team. Since the institute where she worked ran a disabled sports program in conjunction with a small ski resort in Wisconsin, Sandy also took up skiing.

The second time she was on skis, Sandy broke her elbow, ending her first season. And while her first thought was to quit since she didn't want any injuries interfering with her participation on the swim team, the following year she was back on the slopes attending a learn-to-race camp, trading in her swimsuit for a ski suit.

While at a learn-to-race camp in Breckenridge, Colorado, two coaches from Winter Park approached Sandy, inviting her out for the next season. Sandy loved skiing so much she decided to move to Colorado to train full time, putting her career as a social worker in Chicago on hold. Since she already had balance, she could stand and go straight and fast, but didn't do so well turning. In fact, she claims that skiing at first was easy mainly because she was cautious and didn't try anything really challenging. But with the coaching and support from the Winter Park staff, Sandy learned to carve turns around the gates rather than just sliding. And while she's fallen more often since starting to push herself to have better arced turns, she knows that's a sign of progress. After falling a few times, Sandy says it wasn't as scary. And although she's had some bad crashes, Sandy hasn't suffered any major injuries, so she's more comfortable with "pushing the envelope."

After just two and a half years of training at Winter Park, Sandy was selected to be a member of the USDST C team and couldn't stop smiling for more than two weeks. While Sandy mastered the general racing techniques quickly enough to make the Team, she knows she still has a lot of room to grow and credits her quick learning to growing up with a disability, which she says gave her great balance before she even attempted skiing. Sandy also believes she was helped along by her commitment to training full-time and by the excellent coaching and support she received from Winter Park. And while Sandy returns to Chicago for the summer months, her training doesn't stop. She continues to be active with swimming, running, and biking. Making the Team gave Sandy a whole new energy and attitude toward skiing. She says she now runs for fun, but she skis for her life.

Chapter 6
Male Mono-skiers

Chris Devlin-Young is one of the only Disabled Ski Team members to have retired from the Team and made a comeback. He's also the only Team member to win medals as both a stand-up and sit-down skier. And racing in his third Paralympic Games in Salt Lake City at age forty will also make him one of the oldest Team competitors.

In 1982, while on a Coast Guard mission in Alaska's Aleutian Islands, twenty-year-old Chris and his crewmates were attempting to find a runway in the fog. Instead, they found a mountain. Suddenly the view through the windows changed from white to green and the plane crashed into rock. Since he was trained to rescue people, despite some back pain Chris immediately went to work pulling injured crew members out of the burning refuse. Later, at the hospital, X-rays revealed a fractured twelfth thoracic vertebra pushing bone chips into Chris's back. The associated swelling led to paralysis below the level of injury. Chris, who used to run up and down seven thousand-foot mountains from sea level in Alaska, could no longer even wiggle his toes.

For the next two years, Chris felt like half a man and questioned why he was the one so severely injured. He lived at home and did as little as possible. Sleeping, eating, driving around in the car, keeping to himself, and making life miserable for his parents were his main activities. At one point, Chris tried wheelchair basketball but didn't like the hazing new players receive from the seasoned guys. Then one day when Chris was hogging the TV remote in the Palo Alto Veteran's Administration hospital lounge—the usual way he tried to share his mood with everyone else and make their day miserable—a chance meeting with a recreational therapist changed his life.

The therapist asked Chris if he wanted to go skiing through a new program sponsored by the Department of Veterans Affairs and the Disabled American Veterans. Everything would be paid for; all he had to do was come along. Although Chris had never skied, since he had nothing better to do, he decided to give it a try.

At that first clinic held at Alpine Meadows in 1984, Chris and four others from the VA hospital showed up. After two turns in a Mountain Man sit-ski, Chris knew skiing was for him. For the first time since his injury he felt a sense of control over his physical body. And as gravity drew him down the mountain, Chris felt the wind blow through his hair. For Chris, that moment became as monumental as the day he became paralyzed.

Chris was not exactly a natural at skiing. In fact, he fell a lot the first few days. But with many ski instructors from the disabled ski school nearby to help, Chris didn't feel any real frustration. For the next five days, Chris was out on the slopes every day and, on the last day, he had his first chance to try racing. Although he only made it through the first gate of the first run, Chris managed to finish his second run. And while his time didn't win any medals, gaining mastery over his own body and feeling free for the first time in two years was reward enough.

From there, with the encouragement of the ski instructors, Chris naturally progressed through the race circuit. He discovered that with the little control he had of his leg muscles, he could ski standing up using braces and outriggers. For the next 10 years, despite advice from his doctors that he shouldn't, Chris competed in the stand-up category.

In 1985, Chris moved to Winter Park to train at what was then the only disabled race program of its type available in the United States, and competed in enough races to be noticed by the coaches of the USDST. After training for two years, Chris made the Team, living his dream of competing in national and international races. But in 1994, during the Paralympic Games, the doctors' predictions that skiing would tear up his knees came true and Chris was forced to resign himself to a wheelchair and take up mono-skiing.

Once he gave in to sitting down, Chris realized he could actually travel down the road much faster in a wheelchair then he ever could using braces and crutches. It was still a difficult adjustment though, since Chris had felt less paralyzed when standing upright, albeit not always solidly, with the crutches and braces. And once Chris began to mono-ski, he realized he had been crazy to try to stand up and ski. Yet the years as a stand-up skier helped him succeed in a mono-ski. For Chris, struggling to stay standing was a necessary part of his journey, though he'd probably be in a lot less daily pain if he'd sat down long ago.

After retiring from the Team just before the 1998 Nagano Paralympics to pursue other avenues including snowboarding, extreme skiing, and starting up a disabled race-training program at Loon Mountain in New Hampshire, Chris decided to attempt a come-back for the 2002 Paralympics in Salt Lake City. After training for a few months, Chris entered the 2001 World Cup as part of the Winter Park Disabled Team. He placed second in the super G, missing first place by just two one-hundredths of a second. But most important, he ended up third in the overall—enough to show the Team coaches he was back and ready to consistently race and win. In the spring of 2001, he was back on the USDST.

As Chris Devlin-Young was adjusting to life after his injury, Chris Waddell was deciding where to attend college. He chose Middlebury, and became a member of the school's ski team. When he was twenty, Chris planned to spend his first day of Christmas break training at Berkshire East in western Massachusetts. While he was warming up, his ski popped off and the next thing he knew, he was lying on the side of the trail with his brother and a couple of friends standing above him. While Chris remained conscious, he was in shock and remembers nothing of the accident that resulted in near-complete paralysis below his tenth and eleventh thoracic vertebrae.

Chris was taken by ambulance to nearby Franklin County Medical Hospital then airlifted to Hartford Hospital where he underwent surgery to stabilize his back. Following a two-week stay, Chris was transferred to Boston's University Hospital for a six-week course of rehab. During his rehabilitation, no one told him he was paralyzed, so Chris figured he was just injured and would get better. Chris's athlete ego told him things like spinal cord injuries only happened to other people, not to him. With his positive attitude, Chris moved through the most difficult stages of his recovery. But while Chris kept a positive face, as he says, "being in the hospital wasn't very cool," so Chris kept his sights set on one goal—getting back to college.

When friends and family came to visit, to his surprise, Chris found himself putting them at ease. Visitors were generally so uncomfortable and "blown away" by the extent of his injury they didn't have the right words to say. After several weeks of therapy, the head doctor called Chris in for what Chris expected to be a meeting about his discharge. Instead, the doctor, dressed in a coat, tie, and white smock, sat behind his big desk and told Chris he wasn't ready to leave because he hadn't dealt with the depression of being paralyzed. Sitting in his thin cotton hospital johnny, Chris was speechless. Back in his room, Chris told himself he didn't need to deal with depression to get on with his life. Soon he was back home adjusting to his new life in a wheelchair.

Chris resumed an active lifestyle and found both his friends and family not only accepting, but also supportive. That made it easy for Chris to be the same person he had always been. When he did have a bad day, Chris focused on recapturing his life and doing whatever he wanted.

Since Chris had grown up skiing, starting at age three and racing by the age of six, he began to think once again of the ski slopes. He had no idea how he was going to ski, he just knew he was. So when Chris was offered the chance to learn to mono-ski in front of a camera for a documentary on adaptive skiing, he jumped at the opportunity. His ski coach, who had seen the Disabled Team training at Mt. Hood, helped out by getting the Friends of Middlebury Skiing to buy Chris's first mono-ski. Within a year of his accident, Chris was back on the slopes.

Being a skier before his injury, Chris assumed he'd pick up the sport quickly and decided that rather than going through an adaptive program, he'd teach himself. After all, he thought, skiing is skiing. Besides, Chris had the help of his coach and his father, who was a ski instructor. So on his first day back on the slopes, when the coach asked him what he wanted to do, Chris suggested they go to the top of the mountain.

But at the top, Chris soon found himself falling all over the place, unable to make a single turn. By the time he finally did make it to the bottom, he had fallen in ways he'd never fallen before. While pushing along through the lift line, Chris hit a patch of ice with his outrigger and fell, banging his head on a nearby shaft. Adding to his frustration, since Chris had started skiing so young, he didn't remember how he had learned. Each day he came home soaking wet from falling and collecting snow, but excitedly headed to the slopes the next, pleased with his gradual improvement. For Chris, learning how to ski again was learning how to learn. Within three days, Chris was skiing from the top to the bottom of the mountain, and within two weeks, Chris went from being a "never-ever" mono-skier to an advanced intermediate.

Just two weeks later, Chris headed to Winter Park to film the documentary. Once he learned about the Winter Park disabled program, he knew he was being presented with the next step in his recovery. He picked up a schedule of regional qualifying races and competed in his first disabled race the weekend he returned home.

Chris also returned to Middlebury College where he continued his studies in international politics and economics, skied with the college team, and became captain during his senior year, which he viewed as a nice vote of confidence from his friends.

While Chris thought he'd make the Team his first year during the 1990 Nationals at Stratton in Vermont, he fell during the slalom race, usually his best event. Then he was disqualified in the giant slalom when he skied around the last gate. But despite his less-than-perfect performance at Nationals, Chris was invited to participate in the USDST training camps and races. He knew then that if he could show some good results and bide his time, he'd make the Team. The following season, Chris placed second in two races at Winter Park and won two races in Park City in February. At the 1991 Nationals, Chris was appointed to the B Team, just two years after his injury.

During the same years Chris was growing up on the East Coast, Joe Tompkins was becoming an athlete in Alaska. As an adolescent, Joe played baseball, shot hoops, and hung out with his friends. While he was a good baseball player and thought that maybe he could someday play professionally, he took his talent for granted and spent time partying with his friends. When he was nineteen, Joe was a passenger in a car accident involving alcohol which killed his best friend, put another friend in a coma, and left Joe in a wheelchair. Just a month before the accident, Joe's girlfriend had given birth to a son.

Following the accident, Joe struggled with depression and questions of self-worth. He felt unsure about how others perceived him in a wheelchair and the way he perceived himself. To ease his worries and thoughts of not wanting to live, he drank. Two years after the accident Joe realized that if he continued, he was going to have a serious drinking problem and knew he didn't want that to be part of his son's development. If he didn't quit drinking, Joe wouldn't be available for his son, or for anyone else. So he quit.

Around the same time, a friend suggested Joe try skiing, and while he'd only skied a handful of times before, with the help of the Juneau Lion's Club, Joe headed to the slopes. The Lions later sponsored Joe to attend the Ski Spectacular in Breckenridge. Even though Joe finished in last place in the giant slalom there, he saw a sport he could again excel in—and something that might inspire others to take a different path than he had. He returned to Juneau and told the Lions Club that if they would back him, he'd try to make the U.S. Team.

The club backed him as much as it could, and Joe began getting sponsorships on his own. When Joe called Paul DiBello at Winter Park saying he was looking for a place to train, Paul told him to come down. Joe moved to Colorado and trained for the next two and a half years. As he worked out and learned more technical skills, he saw himself move higher in the standings, which brought back the excitement he'd once felt as a competitive athlete. At the 1999 Nationals, the Disabled Team coaches helped Joe out, telling him what he was doing right and what he could do to improve. That gave Joe even more incentive to improve. After the Nationals, Joe made the Team. In addition to being a Team member, Joe has followed through with his commitment to his community's youth. Through speaking engagements and coaching football and Little League, Joe offers kids the helping hand he never had growing up. Through his actions, he shows them there's another way to live life besides partying and alcohol, and emphasizes the importance of setting goals, reaching for them, and not quitting when things get tough.

The same year Chris Devlin-Young's plane crashed, Carl Burnett was born in Cape Elizabeth, Maine. When Carl was just five years old, a car accident changed his life, leaving him partially paralyzed below the second lumbar vertebrae in his lower back. Being so young, Carl adjusted pretty quickly to being in a wheelchair, although for the first few months he resisted doing things for himself. But rather than giving in to Carl's refusals, his parents encouraged him to re-learn to do things for himself so eventually he could become independent.

Since Carl had been skiing since age three, when his father heard about disabled skiing, he suggested his son try it. The year following his accident, Carl was back out on the ski slopes through the Vermont Handicapped Ski Foundation at Mt. Ascutney. He began skiing in a sit-ski, improving progressively over two years, then switched to one of the mono-skis that were just beginning to appear on the slopes. At that point, nine-year-old Carl's skiing began to take off. By age twelve he found out about racing and soon his father was driving him up to Sunday River every weekend to train and race. Carl also became involved in the Alpine Junior Elite Team, a national disabled team funded by the U.S. Olympic Committee. For the next two years, Carl participated in year-round training, attending camps and races all over the country. By the time he reached high school, Carl was ready to commit himself full time to skiing. He enrolled at Gould Academy in Bethel, Maine, where he spent four years skiing at Sunday River every day, a luxury he knew was usually reserved for disabled athletes who chose to train at adaptive programs like Winter Park or Park City.

While Carl had found it generally easy to adapt to life in a wheelchair, being the only disabled skier at the Academy was at times a hassle. While all his classmates got off the bus from school and rushed to get on the mountain to start training, Carl had to find someone to carry his mono-ski upstairs and out to the snow. In general, his coaches and classmates adjusted to having a mono-skier on the team and treated him no differently than the able-bodied skiers.

The next four years, Carl focused on his studies and training and by his senior year, his hard work and training paid off—he made the USDST.

Chapter 7
Arm Amputees, B/K's and "Trash Class"

Some stand-up skiers have never known what it's like not to have a disability. Adam Fromma was born missing the lower part of his right arm and began skiing when he was twelve at Jiminy Peak in Massachusetts. Throughout his childhood, Adam was into skateboarding, but when friends suggested he join them skiing, he went along. At first, skiing was just an occasional pastime. Adam skied only twice that first year, four times the next, and then, in his third year he "got bit" and has loved skiing ever since. Throughout his teen years, Adam skied 70 to 80 times a season. Weeknights he'd ski at nearby Jiminy and on weekends head up to Vermont with his friends.

Until he was twenty, Adam only skied recreationally and knew nothing of the Disabled Team, but a tip from a friend led him to drive out to the Olympic Training Center in Lake Placid where he was given the name of former Team member Paul DiBello. When Adam learned about Paul's racing program at Winter Park he decided to spend the 1995 - 1996 ski season at the NSCD learning to ski gates.

When Adam arrived at the powdery slopes of Colorado, he found he had to scrap everything he knew about skiing and start from the beginning. Growing up on the East Coast, where icy conditions are more the rule than the exception, Adam had learned to ski with a wide stance and lots of edging. While his technique provided stability and worked for recreational skiing, racing fast through softer snow meant narrowing his stance and revising his technique. While he found re-learning to ski frustrating, Adam never thought of giving up. His goal was to make the Disabled Team, and Adam had rarely given up anything in his life—and had a long record of success to prove it.

His biggest setback came in December of 1996, when he tore a ligament in his left knee. As a free skier, Adam had never been injured to the extent that he couldn't get back out on his skis. This time, anxious to get back out and compete, Adam continually pushed himself too far too fast, wrecking his knee repeatedly. Finally Adam gave in to rest and rehab and after six weeks was back out on the slopes. Shortly after that, he made the Team.

Because Adam grew up with his disability, it doesn't affect him much. Other than a slight balance problem, he hasn't even noticed any real

While Csilla feels she benefits greatly from training with able-bodied teams, she sees the added benefit to being part of a disabled ski program where she gets more attention. Able-bodied coaches seem somewhat intimidated by her disability or don't know what to say to her. When she's with the Disabled Team, she feels she gets better coaching, but realizes the able-bodied coaches have many more skiers to deal with so the whole experience naturally is less personal to begin with. Besides, it's difficult for the Academy coaches because Csilla is away so much training with the Disabled Team.

Like other younger members of the Team, Csilla finds juggling ski training and schoolwork a difficult challenge. She gets assignments before she leaves Burke for a race or training camp, then does her homework at night when she has free time—which she admits is not very often. When she's done, she e-mails her assignments back to her teachers. While the system generally works, she admits there have been some "close calls" and that she finds it especially difficult to learn math on her own.

Seventeen-year-old Csilla can't imagine life without skiing. Racing gives her an adrenalin rush and satisfies her competitive nature. Although Csilla feels personally rewarded by skiing and racing, she claims it's not really special—it's just what she does.

While arm amputees generally prefer not to wear a prosthesis skiing, B/K amputees usually do. To watch Clay Fox glide through downhill gates at 60 miles per hour, no one would ever guess he had a disability. Most people don't realize he wears a prosthetic leg since Clay skis with two skis and two poles. Growing up, Clay did some recreational skiing and toyed with racing, but his biggest passion was soccer. He dreamed of playing at the collegiate level.

But when Clay was fifteen, he and some friends were driving back to their hometown of Gillette, Wyoming from a soccer camp in Bozeman, Montana when the driver of the car fell asleep and hit a guard rail sideways going 80 miles per hour. The guardrail came through the car, resulting in Clay's left leg being amputated below the knee. He spent the next two weeks in the hospital, three months in a wheelchair, and another couple of months on crutches before he could walk again. While Clay felt "bummed" for a couple weeks following his injury, he quickly came to accept being an amputee, knowing that as disabilities go, his was pretty minor. Once he was fitted for a prosthesis, Clay resumed his active lifestyle as a varsity soccer player but realized he no longer wanted to pursue the sport beyond high school.

While Clay searched for a new sport to apply himself to, he learned about disabled skiing. Soon Clay was learning to three-track ski at Eagle Mount in Red Lodge Montana until his left leg regained its strength. Through the adaptive program, Clay met other amputees who gave him input on prosthetic legs and being an amputee, and felt grateful for their input. He also learned about the USDST and opportunities in ski racing. When Clay noticed USDST member Greg Mannino on the cover of *Skiing* magazine and read the article describing Greg's accomplishments as an amputee skier, Clay saw a new avenue for his athletic nature.

The following winter, Clay headed out to the NSCD in Winter Park where he learned to ski on two skis wearing a prosthesis. He also fell in love with ski racing. While at Winter Park, the coaches invited him to join their race team, so throughout his sophomore, junior, and senior years in high school, Clay drove out to Colorado for winter training camps. The following year, Clay began college, but after just one semester, he moved to Winter Park to train full time. After four years of training and attending Winter Park's ski camps, Clay accomplished his goal. He was selected for the USDST in the summer of 1998. For Clay, putting on his leg is just like putting on a pair of shoes in the morning. With his prosthesis, he enjoys all the activities he used to enjoy including rock climbing, mountain biking, and running. While every once in a while he'll get an annoying sore on his stump, for him, that's just part of life.

Teammate Mary Ridell also skis with a prosthesis, and has a special ski leg she puts on before hitting the slopes. Before Mary Riddell was born, her mother had Streeter bands, a condition involving rupture of the membrane surrounding her unborn baby. Because of the rupture, fibers from the membrane wrapped around the baby, and while they didn't completely strangle Mary as they sometimes can, they did cut off the circulation to her leg. When Mary was born two-months premature, she was missing her leg below the knee. Despite her amputated limb Mary never considered herself disabled. After all, it was all she had ever known. She got fitted for a prosthesis and because no one pitied her or treated her any differently than the other children, she forgot all about it.

When Mary was four, her parents brought her to the adaptive ski program in Durango, Colorado, not far from their hometown of Dove Creek. By the time Mary was nine, B/K amputee Lana Jo Chapin, an ex-member of the USDST, began coaching Mary in racing. At age ten, Mary knew she wanted to make the Team. Lana Jo told her if she made the choice to pursue racing, she'd have to be dedicated. That meant following through with Lana Jo's instructions and making a lot of sacrifices. Mary quickly made up her mind and dedicated herself 100 percent to skiing. For the next four years, Mary spent most of her weekends on the ski slopes away from friends and family. She didn't attend any school proms or other special events. And while she always knew she could back out if she wanted, she listened to Lana Jo's advice, even when she didn't agree with it. By the time Mary was fourteen, her hard work paid off when she was selected for the Team. Looking back, Mary has no regrets about her sacrifice. In fact, she now approaches all her undertakings "100 percent," never wanting to look back with regret, thinking she could have done something better if only she'd tried harder.

While the medical classification team can usually easily place stand-up skiers into one of the six categories designated for those with arm and leg impairments, the more general nature of some athletes' deficits makes them more difficult to classify. The LW9 class, jokingly referred to by disabled racers as "the trash class," is composed of athletes whose disabilities range from partial paralysis to amputations of an arm and a leg to coordination deficits.

One LW9 is George Sansonetis, who was born in Brooklyn and grew up in upstate New York. He began skiing when he was four and loved being out on the slopes in the fresh mountain air. While attending camp when he was thirteen, George noticed something different about the muscles in his legs and began to have some difficulty walking. But not wanting to miss any activities, he ignored the strange sensation, and didn't tell anyone about it. When his parents noticed his problem when he got home, they brought him to a doctor who concluded his difficulties were due to a strained ligament or torn muscle and sent George through a course of physical therapy. When the problem continued, George's parents brought him to several more doctors who tried numerous treatments, including acupuncture, to no avail. Finally George was sent to a neurologist who diagnosed his problem as dystonia—a rare chronic disease causing involuntary, irregular movements of the body. Since no cure for the condition exists, George was informed he would have to adjust to life with the irregular movements. As the disease progressed,

George noticed that his body involuntarily twisted forward and sideways, especially when he walked.

Despite his progressive difficulty walking and the fact that by the time he was fourteen, he needed crutches just to get around, George continued to ski and noticed that on the slopes, he was actually more independent. By high school, George decided he wanted to compete on his school's ski team, but he didn't get to just walk on to the team as he had hoped. Instead, making the team took a lot of hard work convincing the coaches he could be competitive on the all-able-bodied team. But by his sophomore year, George's persistence paid off. He made the team.

Because George was still on crutches, his coach provided assistance by carrying George's skis to the hill while George worked his way to the lift. There, George would click into his skis, give the crutches to his coach, and be gone up the mountain. Skiing down, he savored the freedom of gravity pulling him down the snow-covered slopes.

But once George made the team, his struggles to succeed were not over. While George just wanted to be treated like all the other athletes, he experienced more than a little frustration because of being perceived as disabled. While coaches gave his teammates specific instructions after each run on how they could improve, George frequently got only good-intended, encouraging words that he was "doing fine." In fact, one coach summed up his opinion of George by saying that he would never really amount to anything as a skier.

George just wanted to be treated like everyone else and to have the chance to pursue his dreams of being a world-class skier. In his heart, he knew he could out-perform his peers' and coaches' low expectations. Fortunately, another coach supported George's efforts and gave him a chance to succeed by telling him what he needed to work on. Those words of encouragement gave George the edge to improve. It was during his high school years that George set his future goals. While attending a career day at school, he told his guidance counselor that his goal was to make the U.S. Ski Team. When his teammates, who were as he says, "consistently kicking his butt" during ski competitions, heard of his plans, they merely chuckled.

After graduating from high school in 1990, George moved to New Mexico where got a series of jobs at Taos Ski Valley. There he continued to pursue the sport he loved. By then, he'd learned to adapt to the involuntary movements of his body and could get around without crutches. Three years later, when a friend gave him the contact information for a disabled ski race happening the following week, George jumped at the chance to compete and show his abilities. He called ahead to register, paid the entry fees and found out what class to enter himself into. On race day, George found himself in a whole new world he'd never known existed.

At that first race, George felt a nervousness he'd never experienced as butterflies invaded his stomach. He knew he didn't have the training and coaching the other disabled racers had. And unlike during high school, this time he was on his own with no one to get his racing bib or help him into his skis. But as he watched the other disabled racers ski down the mountain, George felt inspired. Instead of giving in to his jitters, he kept telling himself he was going to be on the Team. Deep inside, he knew he could become as good as the athletes he watched racing through the gates.

During the 1997 - 1998 ski season, George's dream came true when he was appointed to the Team. With the new factor system just being put into place, George began winning a lot of races because he had one of the largest factors. His wins made others hungry to beat him and knowing he was being chased merely pushed George to race faster. His competitive nature finally got a chance to fully bloom.

Unlike George, teammate Jacob Rife had never skied prior to becoming disabled, and his disability did not appear gradually. One day while walking home from school, ten-year-old Jake sat down on a curb to wait for a semi-truck to go around the corner. The truck happened to catch the curb, jump it, spin forward, and hit him. Jake was rushed to the hospital where he was diagnosed with a spinal cord injury. Luckily, Jake's injury was low down in his back, and he only suffered partial paralysis of both legs—greater on the left side—leaving enough muscle function for him to regain his strength and re-learn to walk. He was left without the ability to flex his left foot, but at least had some control over the rest of his leg muscles.

Although Jake had only skied once before his injury, on a Thanksgiving vacation with his dad, he immediately fell in love with the sport. The year following his accident, Jake's parents got him involved with the disabled ski group at Idaho State University, C.W. Hog, where Jake learned to ski using a brace on his left knee for extra stability. Jake quickly got hooked on skiing and as his interest and abilities grew, he was noticed by one of the able-bodied team coaches who expressed interest in

In Nevada, Allison Pearl also grew up skiing competitively. But when she was eighteen, a freak complication from a blood clot in her leg left her paralyzed below the waist at the level of her fourth and fifth lumbar vertebrae. Over the next month she began to get some sensation back in her thighs, and during the next several weeks Allison slowly regained some leg strength. After three-months of physical therapy she could walk with Canadian crutches and ankle braces. Although the physical and occupational therapists at the rehabilitation hospital told Allison about the great disabled ski program at nearby Alpine Meadows in California, Allison had her sights set on resuming her college studies. And, she didn't want to ski again until she could do it standing up.

Allison had begun skiing and racing when she was five at Sky Tavern, a small area outside Reno. She loved competing and won her first race the same year. During her second year, Allison switched over to Slide Mountain, where she skied for another three years before joining the Squaw Valley Ski Team. When she was thirteen, Allison went to the Junior Olympics, and by the time she was seventeen, she enrolled at the Green Mountain Valley School in Vermont where she could focus on improving her racing skills and complete her high school education. While she planned to compete at the collegiate level, Allison knew her main focus was on attending medical school. With that in mind, she began her studies in biology at the University of Nevada at Reno in the fall of 1993. That's when the blood clot derailed her plans.

But by January, Allison jumped right back into her studies. Although happy to be back at school with many of the friends she'd grown up with, being on crutches felt devastating. While some days Allison didn't really mind the stares and odd looks from people, other days she was overwhelmed with grief.

During her sophomore year, Allison pulled out her old boots and skis and headed to Alpine Meadows to ski standing up. While Allison found that she could stand still alone while holding her poles, she needed someone to hold her waist while she skied down the hill. Still, Allison loved being outdoors doing what she had always loved doing and felt her self-confidence begin to rise again. She skied with assistance several more times until she awoke to a fresh powder day and a foot and a half of new snow. When Allison arrived at the mountain, her instructor looked at her, read her mind, and knew she wanted to be swooping down the mountain.

To do that, her instructor said, she'd have to get into a mono-ski. Without a second thought, Allison conceded.

While Allison found it a bit challenging learning how to maneuver the unfamiliar ski and fell frequently, she loved being back under her own control. For the first time in months, she was having real fun. By mid-day, she was linking turns and skiing to the bottom without falling. Within a day and a half she moved, untethered, off the bunny slope to an intermediate run.

Although Allison enjoyed being back on the slopes, she still didn't consider returning to racing. She was in the midst of applying to medical school and thought she'd just be a recreational skier. So instead of improving her skiing, she took the next two and a half seasons off, skiing only once or twice for fun. During her first year in medical school at the University of Nevada, she skied once, but continued her focus on her studies. But during the second year, she heard about a race at nearby Mount Rose, the first disabled race on the West Coast in four years. That year she'd done more recreational skiing as an outlet from her stressful studies, and thought it would be fun to try racing again.

When she arrived at the starting gate for the race, Allison felt the familiar exciting butterflies racing in her stomach and noticed her competitive spirit resurface. From that one race, Allison qualified to go to the Nationals in Breckenridge. Leery of the mind-games she remembered in able-bodied ski racing, Allison began training for the event. To her surprise, instead of feeling burned out by racing as she had back in high school, Allison was again in love with skiing and found she could easily balance competition with her medical studies. As she got more involved with racing, she realized she'd love to make the U.S. Disabled Team, and planned a six-week reprieve from medical school to train at Winter Park. As soon as she arrived, she competed in Park City's Huntsman Cup, where she surprised herself by winning the slalom. Although she went on to compete in the Nationals, she fell in two events and got just one medal in another. During the next season, Allison took a full two months off from school to devote more time to racing. That year, she won the gold in the Huntsman Cup super G, a silver in the giant slalom, and a gold in slalom. She continued on to medal at the Columbia Crest Cup in Winter Park, and just after the 2001 Nationals she was named to the disabled A Team, which was a huge honor since most Team members begin on the C Team. After completing her medical degree that May, Allison landed a research position in Palo Alto, California to study Alzheimer's and Multiple Sclerosis.

Around the time Muffy decided she would grow up to be an Olympic champion, Lacey Heward was born in another Idaho community. When Lacey was just sixteen months old, she and her four-year-old brother headed outside to play in the dirt by their home in the country. While playing near a weight bench, her brother decided to take one side of the weights off the barbell. Suddenly the other side slipped off and struck Lacy in the back, pinching her spine.

Following the incident, doctors performed open spinal cord exploratory surgery to determine if Lacey had sustained any injury and sent her through a course of physical therapy where she learned to walk using braces and crutches. But it soon became apparent that because of the spinal cord injury, some of her muscles were paralyzed. Without a good balance of strength between the thigh muscles surrounding her joints, Lacey's stronger muscles pulled her hips out of their sockets. Doctors informed her parents that if Lacey was ever going to walk normally, her hips would have to be put back into place.

When she was six, her family moved to Utah and Lacey went to Shriners Hospital in Salt Lake City to undergo surgery. When the first surgery failed, she went in a second time and was put into a body cast for six months to stabilize her hips. But despite her doctor's best efforts, the surgery failed once again. Over time, the tendons in her leg tightened and Lacey could no longer completely straighten her leg. By the time she was nine, Lacey was in a wheelchair.

Since her family had always treated her like any other child, Lacey knew nothing about being in a wheelchair. For the first two years she used a heavy hospital wheelchair, but when she began going to physical therapy back in Idaho the therapists got her a lighter sports chair. It was then Lacey realized she'd better adapt to being in a chair, although she never gave up her goal of walking again and faithfully continued to exercise and stretch her legs.

When her father, who was by then divorced from her mother, found out about adaptive skiing, he told Lacey about it. Although it sounded like fun and she really wanted to try it, her family didn't have the money to get her started. But by the time she was fourteen, Lacey found out about a fundraising program to get her involved with the Recreation Unlimited program at Bogus Basin, Idaho. Lacey went door to door selling raffle tickets to earn her lessons and was soon out on the mountain in a mono-ski.

The first day, the instructors brought Lacey onto a bunny hill and helped her ski using a tether. Lacey, who had grown up being active with her four sisters and one brother, hated being limited by the tether. And she was frustrated with falling. She told herself she would learn to ski that day so she could go untethered and move on to a bigger slope. If she didn't, she wasn't going to ski anymore. By the end of the day, Lacey could successfully link turns down the hill.

When one of the instructors approached her and asked her if she wanted to be in a race the following day, Lacey quickly declined. The only thing she knew about racing was from watching the Olympics on TV. While Lacey had started skiing to be active again with her family, as her skiing skills improved the comments she received gave her an unexpected reward. Instead of a nice pat on the back and comments to the effect that it was cool that a disabled person could ski, Lacey realized people looked up to her because she was a good skier. For the first time in ages, she felt like she was equal. With her success on the slopes, she realized she could do anything she set her mind to. While over the next few months instructors encouraged her to race, it wasn't until the following year that Lacey finally tried her first gates.

When Lacey entered high school, some of the teachers heard that she skied and invited her to join the school team. Although she was the only disabled skier on the team, and wasn't very good, she really enjoyed the sport and learned some basic racing skills which prepared her for the First Security (now Wells Fargo) Winter Games of Idaho. At the Games, despite feeling nervous, she loved the whole experience of wearing a bib and competing. Although, as one of the few disabled skiers, she didn't have much competition, she was happy just being able to finish a run, and took home a few gold medals. For the next three years, the Games were the highlight of her season. And each year Lacey loved to see herself improve. But after high school, without a team, Lacey wasn't sure what to do. Although she wanted to have her own mono-ski, they were much too expensive for her to afford, so she put her skiing aside and studied jazz music for a year at Mt. Hood Community College. When she realized that despite her love of music, she didn't want to be part of the music scene, Lacey decided she'd go into motivational speaking. But to do that, she needed something to talk about. Acting on blind faith, when Lacey was eighteen she got a local company in Boise to sponsor her, packed her bags, and moved to Utah to train with the National Ability Center in Park City.

Lacey moved in with her sister and got a part-time job in a dental office, then lucked into connecting with an older woman who wanted to sponsor Lacey's skiing. So with her skis, entry fees, and travel taken care of, Lacey set about following her training schedule. At Park City, she got to hang around with team member Chris Waddell, whom she admired greatly. Chris and all the other disabled skiers she trained with helped motivate her and push her along. Lacey's training began to pay off. She came in third at her first Columbia Crest Cup. And later, at the Nationals in Vermont, she took second in slalom and third in downhill.

But being the type of person who starts things and then stops, by following year, Lacey didn't want to ski anymore. In the fall of 2000, while everyone else was out training for the upcoming season, Lacey just wanted to quit. She'd look at the poster in her room that said "2002 Olympics" and instead of feeling excited, she just felt scared. Feeling the mounting pressure and afraid of failure, she'd hit a wall. At some level, she knew she wouldn't really quit for good, but it took the encouragement of her coach to get her back out on the mountain.

By then it was January and the Huntsman Cup was less than a month away. Even though Lacey showed up on the slopes, she brought a negative attitude with her. The first day, she hurt her shoulder and didn't want to go back up the next day. Instead of feeling excited about the upcoming race, she just went home crying, frustrated, and mad. After she let out all her frustration, Lacey said a little prayer, reminded herself of why she was skiing, and told herself she could do it. She knew she had a greater purpose than just skiing and that by becoming an elite athlete, she could help others. After that, she was fine.

At her first World Cup event, held at Snowbasin, Utah in early March 2001, Lacey placed fifth in the GS and fourth in the slalom, racing against the world's best mono-skiers. But Lacey wasn't even worried about placing, she was just excited to be at her first international event. The following week, at the Canadian World Cup, she won the slalom. Then, following the 2001 Nationals at Big Sky, Montana, Lacey received a letter from Coach Ewald. She was on the Team.

Photo Gallery

Andy Parr and Diana Golden-Brosnihan

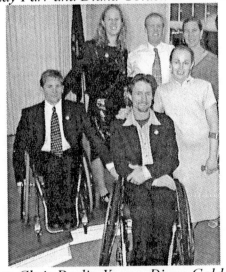

Front - Carl Burnett, Chris Devlin-Young, Diana Golden-Brosnihan. Back - Sarah Billmeier, Andy Parr, Jennifer Zanca (former USDST Program Manager)
Photos by Bob Stevens

71

Chris Devlin-Young, Andy Parr, and Monte Meier
Photo by Bob Stevens

Greg Mannino
Photo by Selko Photography

Chris Devlin-Young on mono-board
Photo by Sport Obermeyer

Mountain Man Bi-Ski Being Tethered
Photo by Mountain Man

Allison Jones
Photo by Big Sky Montana

Jake Rife
Photo by Selko Photography

George Sansonetis
Photo by Selko Photography

Csilla Kristof
Photo by Dr. Mike Messner

Csilla Kristof
Photo by Dr. Mike Messner

Lee Joiner
Photo by Mike Messner

Muffy Davis
Photos by Jonathan Selkowitz,
Selko Photography, Jackson
Hole, Wyoming

Allison Pearl

Danny Kosick
Photo by Dr. Mike Messner

Chapter 9
Behind the Scenes

It's 3 a.m. and Vinnie Poch is already preparing for the day's race. After taking snow temperatures and humidity readings, Vinnie settles into helping the Team's ski technician, Mark Canfield, sharpen and wax each team member's skis for the day's race conditions. Throughout the day as temperatures and snow conditions change, they will modify the ski wax so skiers running later will have an equal chance at a winning race. "It's more than just skiing that wins a race," explains Vinnie, who sees his role as equipment manager as a vital component to the success of the USDST. Before each run, Vinnie and Mark will sometimes apply speed overlays— rub-on waxes that provide extra speed in wetter snow and keep the skis fresh for the second run.

Vinnie began his job with the USDST in 1999 when coach Ray Watkins asked him to fill the recently vacated position. Ray was already familiar with Vinnie's work since the two had met at Mt. Shasta, California years before when Vinnie attended Ray's ski camps. Vinnie's eight years of experience tuning skis at a local shop prepared him well for his new job.

Vinnie travels with the Team to all the major races and helps out at the ski camps, where he gets to sleep a bit later. During camps, Vinnie leaves the house at 6 a.m. to pick up team members, load their wheelchairs into the car, and bring them to the training hill. Throughout the day Vinnie helps set courses and makes sure everyone has everything they need. Despite the early mornings, long hours, and hard work, Vinnie says he likes working with the disabled team where everyone is like family. "These guys are just awesome," Vinnie says. "They're not pretentious, just regular folks."

Vinnie is just one of the supporting staff who works behind the scenes of the USDST. Along with the four coaches and the other support staff, Vinnie helps make the Team the number one disabled ski team in the world.

Until he retired at the end of the 2001 ski season, alpine coordinator Steve "Stoney" Stone, was the guy who made sure everyone on the Team got to the many races each year. While the athletes generally book their own flights to and from races, Stoney took care of getting the best lodging deals and carefully arranged room assignments to avoid personality conflicts. Planning travel for as many as 35 people involves a lot of paperwork, as do the rest of the tasks involved with planning and running a disabled ski team. As an emergency medical technician (EMT), Stoney also kept track of any health problems and consulted doctors if anything serious arose.

Fifty-four-year-old Stoney began his involvement with the Team back in the early 1970's. As a Vietnam veteran, when he returned to Winter Park following the war and began working as a ski patroller, he naturally gravitated toward other veterans. After doing photography for the Team in an adopted role, he began officially working as the Team photographer in 1984. The job evolved to being the start coach, then later into a managerial role. Like other staff members, Stoney enjoyed being around the Team and says he and the other staff look at the Team members' athletic abilities first, and notice their disabilities second. In fact, Stoney says there are a lot of times he doesn't even see the disabilities anymore. Although Stoney will no longer be formally working with the Team, he plans to keep in touch with all the athletes that he has, in a sense, helped raise over the years. His responsibilities will be shared between Head Coach Ewald Zirbisegger and staff member Aaron Norman.

Aaron began his affiliation with the USDST as a guide for blind skier Bobby McMullen. Like Vinnie, Aaron skied at Mt. Shasta, and met Bobby on the slopes years before. When Bobby needed a new guide following his success at the 1998 Nagano Paralympics, Aaron was happy to step into the role. While it was at first a challenge to guide Bobby —Bobby has no vision in his left eye and only 20/1200 in his right—Aaron quickly learned the skills of pre-race preparation and guiding Bobby through the gates. The team worked together for two and a half years, until Bobby was forced to retire from the Team because of health issues. Since he was already familiar with the Team members, Aaron easily stepped into the roles of start coach and assistant strength and conditioning coach.

While not the most visible job, the start coach plays one of the most important roles in a ski race. Aaron takes care of all the pre-race issues for the athletes once they enter the start house at the top of the racecourse. This requires knowing the unique personalities and pre-race routines of each racer. Prior to every racer's start, Aaron makes sure he or she is warm and has clear goggles. He keeps spare goggles and lenses on hand in case of emergencies. Some racers have Aaron give their legs a rubdown to get them warm. For others, like B/K amputee Mary Riddell, Aaron stands in front to block their view so they don't see the athletes in front of them leave the start. Aaron may also help athletes focus on their breathing to keep them relaxed and calm. Aaron also checks each skier's equipment to make sure all the components are working properly. For mono-skiers this means making sure a metal pin is inserted in the ski binding to prevent it from releasing, otherwise the extra forces a mono-skier puts on the binding can often make it release prematurely. And for skiers using outriggers, Aaron checks the release mechanism to ensure it will work properly when the racer goes out of the gates.

Another part of Aaron's role is to listen to race reports through a small earpiece and feed information to athletes interested in knowing about changing terrain or conditions. Most of the reports come from the coaches who watch the racers in action from various points along the course, but some feedback comes from the racers themselves. While some skiers like to hear about changing conditions, others, like three-tracker Jason Lalla, generally don't want to hear any course reports or get any input from Aaron. Instead, Jason prefers to go through his whole start routine without interruption.

Knowing each athlete well is critical. Although Aaron already had a good rapport with the athletes through his role as a guide, he didn't know everyone's start routines. When he began his job, he met with former start coach Ray Watkins to learn what worked and what didn't for each athlete. Then he spent a week meeting with each team member to learn his or her pre-race routines. The transition was made easier since the athletes already knew and trusted Aaron. As Aaron explains, each athlete has their own idiosyncrasies and it's critical for them to keep to their normal routine. Some racers arrive at the start gates early and go through a whole routine of stretching and listening to music. Others show up right before the race and head out the gates. The important thing is that each athlete stick with his or her own routine. "If they go out of their routine it's hard for them," Aaron explains. "They want everything to be in order and just the way they like it before they head out to get into their individual zones."

Sometimes Aaron plays an even more important role in settling down a frazzled skier. When Jennifer Kelchner arrived late for her start during the 2001 U.S. Nationals and, Aaron says was going "a million miles an hour," Aaron calmed her down and she had a good run.

When wearing his other hat as assistant strength and conditioning coach, Aaron works alongside coach Ray Watkins overseeing all the aspects of the Team members' physical training. This involves setting up individualized exercise programs and modifying the programs as necessary. If athletes have particular questions about their workouts, or want a more personalized program to work on a specific area, the coaches take them to the gym and work with them on an individual basis. On days off, Aaron will sometimes organize a team bike ride or other activity.

Ray Watkins also began his career with the USDST as a blind guide, skiing with Brian Santos for the 1990 Nationals in Bend, Oregon. At the time, Ray was running Mt. Shasta's ski program as well as the local junior college's ski program. Ray stepped into the role of start coach in 1999 and later became in charge of conditioning.

During pre-season training each summer and fall, Ray is responsible for developing individualized workouts for all the athletes based upon a lactate threshold evaluation, which includes tests of heart rates, training zones, and recovery heart rates. During camps, the entire team works on core conditioning and strengthening in the gym. The progressive exercise program includes a warm up session, sitting and standing on Swiss balls to increase core stability and strength, additional balance work using a Dynadisk, and weight lifting. A goal file is kept for each athlete with short-term, season, and long-term goals. Before training in the gym, the athletes head to the slopes for work on skiing fundamentals, carefully watched by the coaches who check to be sure the athletes move everything down the hill in a flexed stance while keeping dynamic balance. Ray also works with the athletes on mental preparation for races, which he says is an optional part of training.

Like Vinnie, Ray prefers to work with disabled athletes, finding the work offers more variety and challenge. "With able-bodied you have a certain kind of protocol with the athletes," Ray explains. "You're looking at the same things, but with disabled you're always looking at someone who has a different way of accomplishing things."

Coach Chris Griffin, known as "Griff," agrees. He says the main reason he enjoys his work with the Team is the atmosphere. "You can coach 'normies' and they're all pretty much cookie cutters," he says. "With the disabled team, nobody is the same—not even close." Even though every skier, disabled or able-bodied, has to make the ski do the same things, the trick is in how they get it done. And since every disability is different, each team member develops his or her own unique technique.

As a former USDST member and later a coach for the Bear Valley Junior Ski Team, Griff naturally assumed his role of USDST coach in 1998. Griff started skiing at age three in Minnesota and later skied at Mammoth and June Mountains in California. He became interested in racing when he was nineteen and raced until he lost his right arm and shoulder in a construction accident when he was thirty. After Griff spent two years being angry, a friend introduced him to the Far West Disabled Ski Team and Griff rediscovered the joy of racing, soon achieving his new goal of landing a spot on the USDST. Griff medalled in the giant slalom in the 1992 Paralympic Games, but after an anterior cruciate ligament (ACL) replacement in his knee and more knee problems in 1994, he decided to retire from racing. That's when he began coaching, first for the Bear Valley able-bodied team, then applying his skills and knowledge to the USDST. Unlike other coaches who are available for the Team year-round, Griff chooses to be an "on-the-hill guy," only participating in snow training and races. This schedule allows him time to spend with his wife and be involved with other pursuits like golf and spending time on his ranch.

In addition to setting courses and giving skiers feedback at training camps, Griff works alongside coach Kevin Jardine using a digital video camera to film the athletes training and racing. At races, they also take footage of the top racers from other countries. They then use a computer to make individualized CDs that include video clips of the athlete and his or her main rivals who have a similar disability. The clips serve as valuable tools for comparison, allowing the athletes to see what they are doing right and identify areas of weakness. Griff and Kevin then come up with specific exercises to add to each athlete's gym routine to strengthen weak areas.

Kevin grew up ski racing in Canada and the United States and began coaching in a small town outside Buffalo, New York at age sixteen as a way to afford the expense involved in ski racing. He soon discovered his passion for coaching and retired from racing at age nineteen after a crash in which he injured his back. The following year, Kevin enrolled at the University of Toronto where he majored in kinesiology with an emphasis on coaching. Following school, he applied for many coaching positions around North America, but felt drawn to a position at the National Sports Center for the Disabled in Winter Park, even though he had never even seen a disabled skier before. By 1998 Kevin was named Head Coach and that same year was asked to be the head coach of the New Zealand Disabled Ski Team. Although the New Zealand team had only five athletes, they won seven medals in the 1998 Nagano Paralympics, including five gold. The next season, Canada, Germany and the United States all offered him positions. Since working with the best possible team and staff has always been an emphasis for Kevin, he chose to work with the USDST.

Kevin summarizes his role as guidance counselor, conditioning coach and teacher. "We take the skills the skiers have now and we try to refine them and make them faster," he says. In addition to video analysis, Kevin helps manage equipment, organizes competition at able-bodied races, coordinates development camps and represents the Team on the Alpine Competition Committee. He also spends many hours in front of the computer during training camps and races, entering the day's results, working on schedules, and communicating and updating the USSA media department.

Kevin also finds coaching disabled racers more interesting than able-bodied athletes because of each individual skier's needs. And, he says, it's fun because the athletes have a lot of desire. "It's something they can be competitive at and they actually improve at a much faster rate than an able-bodied skier because of that desire to get good," he says.

Head Coach Ewald Zirbisegger agrees that coaching disabled and able-bodied is basically the same, whether you have one or two legs or a mono-ski. "You make the ski turn right or left, go straight down the mountains, that's all you really do," he says. Ewald, who grew up racing in Austria, raced for his homeland's national team for a dozen years before injuries kept him out of the 1980 Olympics in Lake Placid. That same year, he moved to Winter Park and raced professionally for several seasons in the United States and Japan before joining the staff at Winter Park's disabled program. When he retired from racing in 1993, Ewald was asked to be a guest coach for the USDST and later assumed the role of head coach.

Since speed events have always been Ewald's favorites, he and the other coaches have been pushing the Team to go faster. "We're setting up more speed camps in our training," he says, adding that year-round conditioning helps tremendously, as well as believing in yourself and trusting you can win. He compares ski racing to any job where skills must be done repeatedly until they become automatic without much thinking involved.

While Ewald and the other coaches push the athletes really hard both on and off the slopes, they always keep safety in mind. "We don't want to bang up our girls and guys," he says. "They're already banged up. But we push them to get better." And the coaching they provide gets results. "When you see a mono-skier in a downhill course do 35 yards air time and land skiing 65 miles per hour," Ewald says, "it's pretty impressive."

Since his involvement, Ewald has witnessed the Team become more professional both on and off the slopes and believes the training they receive as members of the USDST will benefit them throughout their lives.

While not as visible, many former Team members continue to play key roles in the development and success of disabled ski racing. Colorado resident Jack Benedick now gives back to the sport that benefited his life by serving on the Board of Directors for the U.S. Ski Team. He also serves on the International Paralympic Committee. Jack, who retired from working formally for the USDST in 1995, has evolved with the Team. As a disabled Vietnam veteran who lost both his legs in 1969 when he stepped on a mine, Jack got involved with skiing in the early days of the Team. At that time, there were no standards to follow. Just showing up at a race was enough to qualify. Early on, Jack became involved with running the Team and became the Competition Director for the National Handicapped Sports and Recreation Association, which later became DS/USA, and he continued to take on various roles as the sport grew. Nowadays, Jack is often seen at races, inspecting courses and cheering the Team on.

Bob Maserve, who raced with the Team from 1990 to 1994, also continues to stay close to the Team that made a big difference in his life. Since retiring from the Team, Bob has stayed involved as a mentor. He represents disabled athletes on various boards, serving as vice-president of DS/USA and working on a fundraising advisory group. Beyond the slopes, Bob says what he learned as a USDST member helped him grow into his career as a senior manager for a commercial contractor. "You don't see many people in a wheelchair in a management position in construction," he says.

Chapter 10
Training

Once a disabled skier makes the U.S. Team, his or her hard work in many ways has only just begun. For B/K amputee Mary Ridell and other members of the Team, training season never really ends. During the summer Mary trains three to four days a week in the gym where she completes a program designed by a sports physiologist. Each workout lasts about an hour and 20 minutes. While Mary used to workout for longer periods, she's cut back since research is finding that maximum effort starts to deplete after about 55 minutes. When she was younger, Mary did most of her training by actually skiing, following the philosophy that good ski racing comes from putting in lots of miles on the hill. Now she spends time both on the hill and in the gym, balancing quantity with quality. Since after several years of ski racing Mary's muscles are programmed pretty well, she's also shifted some of her attention toward the mental aspects of winning by reading a lot of books about mental training and sports. Many of her teammates and coaches agree that the mental aspect of training is equally as important as, if not more important than, the physical aspects. To bring herself to a higher level, Mary also competes in able-bodied events throughout the ski season. These competitions push her beyond the limits of skiing with other disabled skiers and bring her disabled racing to a higher level.

Physical and mental training make up only part of what is required to win races. Another important aspect is goal setting. As mono-skier Chris Waddell explains, goal setting involves not just making a goal, but also figuring out how to achieve it by breaking it down into intermediate steps that don't seem so intimidating.

When Chris achieved his goal of making the Team, he set another goal—to be the world's fastest mono-skier. To reach that goal, he relocated from the East Coast to Vail, Colorado and also changed some of his equipment. Because Chris doesn't have stomach and back muscles, he got a bucket for his mono-ski with a higher backrest and wrapped an elastic kidney belt from his sternum to his belly button for added stability. But Chris knew that winning races was about more than the right equipment. The key element of his training would be skiing. He skied more often and forced himself to ski on more difficult terrain, including more bumps. Chris found the perfect training run at Vail and taught himself how to be comfortable catching air by going as fast as he could over the bumps. His technical skills improved along with his balance. And besides building his confidence, Chris found skiing the more challenging run was fun. Combining his own training time with the hours spent at camp with the coaches, Chris watched himself move toward his goal.

In the summers, what began as dry land training resulted in a second athletic career as a wheelchair racer, which eventually took Chris to the summer Paralympics. During the summer, Chris puts in 60 to 120 miles per week in his wheelchair and works out in the gym three to four days. Over time, his training evolved from focusing on how much he could lift to using lighter weights while sitting on a bench with no back support to work on improving his balance.

Recently Chris started doing more stability training on a Swiss ball where he tries to engage as many of his functional trunk muscles as he can to make up for the ones he's missing. In disabled sports, athletes often compensate for weakened muscles with stronger ones. While some spinal cord injured athletes actually lift weights while sitting on the ball—an activity that challenges trunk strength and balance and improves stability—Chris gets a good workout from just sitting on the ball and maintaining his balance.

Although Chris is now one of the top mono-skiers in the world, he continues to show up at all the training camps, knowing that to maintain his position, he must keep training hard. In fact, once an athlete is named to the A, B, or C Team, he or she must continue to meet all the requirements each year or get dropped down to the next level. And once any skier makes the Team, he or she only has two years to prove his or her willingness and ability to meet the demands of training, racing, and being competitive. Head Coach Ewald has even been known to take tickets to an upcoming race back from racers if they aren't doing well during the season. While Ewald doesn't enjoy doing it, and the skiers don't enjoy losing their tickets, it does succeed in pushing skiers to improve their performance.

The A/K amputees of the LW2 class, who usually have four or five members on the team during any one season, have the added advantage during training of competing against each other for a limited number of racing spots. Dan Kosick thinks that because of this, the amputees improve quicker than the other classes and become better prepared for the bigger races. The LW2s are very competitive, and on any given day, any of them can win. Yet the LW2s are also all great friends. When Jason Lalla made the team, he looked up to Monte Meier as a mentor. Although Monte is Jason's competitor, he lends Jason wax, helps him tune his skis, and actually gave him one of his skis to use for a while. That type of support is prevalent throughout the team, where senior team members willingly help the up-and-coming athletes. But, at the starting gate of a race, ski racing again becomes an individual sport, and according to Jacob Rife, on race day team members have even been known to "psych each other out a bit."

George Sansonetis, who also trains throughout the summer, often thinks about something Ewald told him—that races are won in the summer, not the winter. By building up his strength during the summer, he figures he's got much of the battle won already. George spends time both in the gym strength training and outside mountain biking to build more strength and endurance. And come ski season, he's back on the slopes training in addition to his workouts.

Besides the athlete's individual training program, the team meets several times a year for dry land and on-the-slopes training camps. After the official race season was over in 2001, the team headed to Arapahoe Basin in Colorado for over a weeks' training. Then, as during other summers, the team headed to Mount Hood in Oregon for snow training camps. There, racers begin their day at 6 a.m., running gates or drills on the snow, break for a couple hours to eat lunch and rest, then spend the afternoon in the gym riding exercise bikes, lifting weights, and working on core conditioning. After training, they eat and go to bed, resting up to repeat the schedule the next day.

At the Mount Hood camp, the athletes receive a standardized training schedule, which dictates their work for the summer. The athletes' training is also dictated by the results of tests performed each fall at the Orthopedic Specialty Hospital in Salt Lake City, Utah.

In past years, the Team has also held dry land-only camps at the U.S. Olympic Training Center in Colorado Springs and at Lake Placid, New York. At these camps, team members lift weights, do calisthenics and stretches, and put in lots of time in the pool. Games like basketball, water polo, water basketball, softball, soccer, and Frisbee round out the training.

For Muffy Davis, dealing with performance anxiety has been a big part of training and becoming a better racer. Muffy always used to put pressure on herself to perform—not just for herself, but for her family, her sponsors, the team, and her entire hometown of Sun Valley. Working with a sports psychologist, who assured Muffy her supporters love her whether she wins four medals or none and that her sponsors are backing her because they know what she's capable of and want her to achieve her dreams, has lessened Muffy's performance anxiety. Instead of focusing on the bad snow conditions, the amount of competition, or the intimidation of the Paralympics, Muffy now focuses on having fun and just skiing her best. And, Muffy reminds herself of the Olympic Creed, which she feels America has lost sight of with so much focus on money, marketing and getting endorsements. The Olympic Creed states, "The most important thing in the Olympic Games is not to win but to take part, just as the most important thing in life is not the triumph, but the struggle. The essential thing is not to have conquered, but to have fought well." Just making it to the Paralympics is exceptional. After all, Muffy says, even if a skier comes in fourth at an international competition, it means they're fourth in the world, and that's pretty damn good.

Chapter 11
Funding

The hard work and dedication required to make the USDST does not end once a racer makes the Team. In addition to year-round training both on and off the hill, obtaining funding to support their career becomes an ongoing challenge for many Team members. Annual costs for travel, lodging, food, equipment and race fees during the 2000 - 2001 ski season ranged around $5,000 and can go upwards of $10,000 for those requiring more expensive equipment and choosing to enter more races. Depending upon team placement (A, B, or C) some or all of these expenses are covered by the USDST, but even A Team members must meet their usual housing and food expenses when they are not training or racing with the Team. As mono-skier Chris Waddell says, "Eating and sleeping are pretty important things."

Fortunately, athletes usually manage to meet these expenses through a combination of private and corporate sponsorships, scholarships, and creative fundraising events. Gaining the people skills necessary to approach and obtain potential sponsors becomes an added benefit to being a Team member that helps racers long after they retire from the Team.

USDST members named to the C Team must come up with 75 percent of their travel expenses to scheduled events, or about $3,500. The USDST covers the remaining 25 percent. If racers choose to enter additional races, they are responsible for 100 percent of all costs. B Team members must cover 50 percent of their expenses, while for A Team members, all travel expenses are covered. For visually-impaired athletes, the funding challenge doubles since they must cover their guides' expenditures in addition to their own.

Team members must obtain their own equipment including skis, poles, boots, and goggles. Equipment manufacturers who agree to sponsor an athlete provide gear, but getting sponsorships is often difficult. While the average recreational skier can generally get away with one or two pairs of skis, Team members like Adam Fromma may have eight or more. Especially for technical events, Adam uses both training and racing skis of different lengths to accommodate varying snow conditions and different course set-ups. He decides which pair to run on depending upon who sets the course, the terrain, and how open a course is. His training skis get beat up during the year, but in the start area, he clicks off the training skis and steps into a pair of freshly tuned and waxed racing skis chosen for the particular racecourse. While Adam owns only one pair of ski boots, he replaces these every year to make sure they are stiff. Skiing 180 days a season softens boots very quickly.

Besides the equipment expense, daily lift ticket costs and food easily exceed $50 at many ski areas. In this area, having a physical impairment offers an advantage. Adaptive ski programs generally offer reduced-cost lift tickets, equipment rentals, and lessons for people with disabilities and at least one program offers skiing free-of-charge. And some disabled ski advocates are working to require areas to offer free lift tickets to the ski guides necessary for some disabled skiers.

Athletes come up with many ways to fund their ski careers. In the early stages of learning to ski and race, parents often pay for skiing and some adaptive programs organize fundraisers to help youth pay their way. Mono-skier Lacey Heward remembers going door to door selling raffle tickets when she was fourteen to pay for her skiing through Recreation Unlimited, an Idaho program offering adaptive lessons at Bogus Basin. Since making the U.S. Team in the spring of 2001, Lacey started working on getting corporate sponsors. Larry Miller Sundance Dodge, an Idaho auto dealer, held a sale during the month of July, with a portion of the profits from each car sale going to support Lacey's ski racing.

Many of the athletes hold down summer jobs. Arm amputee Adam Fromma paints houses, a job that allows him the flexibility to attend summer training camps. But the busy racing and training season from fall to spring makes working during the season difficult. Athletes might be home for one or two weeks, then away for up to a month at a time. During the 2000 - 2001 ski season, amputee skier Jason Lalla counted the days he was at home in Vail between October and April. The total came to 30.

Obtaining sponsorships is one way disabled athletes, like their able-bodied counterparts, try to pay for their racing careers. Occasionally a company calls the Team asking for an athlete to sponsor, which is how Jacob Rife got Visa as his main sponsor, but usually the athletes must put in many hours of work to obtain a sponsor.

B/K amputee Clay Fox, whose parents helped him a lot when he was on the B and C Teams, says he lucked into sponsorships when he made the A Team. In his experience, getting sponsorships mostly comes down to knowing someone who's willing to help out, or knowing someone who knows someone and being in the right place at the right time. Challenged

Athletes, a California organization that provides funds to disabled athletes and funds many USDST members, is just one of Clay's sponsors. Like many other amputees, Clay gets his ski leg through a prosthetic company sponsor who also gives him money to help defray race expenses.

For amputee skier Dan Kosick, the idea of becoming a ski racer and traveling to New Zealand and Colorado with the Winter Park disabled program gave him the incentive to raise funds himself. His first fundraiser, a spaghetti dinner, was a huge success. Since Dan's parents were both divorced and remarried and divorced again, he had lots of family, including grandparents, willing to help him organize the event. Dan's father's best friend owned a restaurant and agreed to put the spaghetti dinner on for free. They charged $10 a plate. The all-day event, which included raffles for prizes donated by local businesses, was very well attended and raised $10,000, allowing Dan to buy ski clothes and equipment and to attend the Winter Park camps the following year. But, Dan soon learned that much of the heavy designer ski clothes he purchased weren't necessary since racers wear specially designed lightweight ski suits.

Since his first successful fundraiser, Dan continues to work hard to attract sponsors and obtain funding, often with help from local businesses and community members. A woman who runs the local shopping mall donates money each year and connects Dan with others in the community who provide prizes for his events. One year a mall shop donated Beanie Babies for a raffle set up by the local semi-pro hockey team. But Dan's favorite fundraising event is the annual golf tournament at Belden Hill in upstate New York.

While the golf tournament has become his biggest and most successful fundraiser, Dan enjoys it most because unlike at other events, he doesn't feel like he's begging. Rather than just giving Dan money and walking away, people pay to come to play golf all day, enjoy a steak dinner, and win prizes—and Dan earns the money he needs to ski. With the golf tournaments, Dan created a recipe for successful fundraising. In 2000, 23 teams of four players showed up (a typical full tournament consists of just 18 teams). In addition to receiving the entry fees, Dan obtains money from sponsors in exchange for displaying company logos on the greens. Sponsors also donate prizes and raffle items.

Despite his success at fundraising and the fact that he looks forward to the annual golf tournament, Dan admits it takes a lot of time and effort away from what he'd really like to be doing—racing. Whenever he's got time away from his training schedule, Dan goes to all the local businesses and asks for prize donations. Dan's sponsors include Oakley eyewear, Atomic skis, and Cold Fusion Foods, a relatively new company based on the West Coast that manufactures healthy popsicles containing protein and vitamins. He landed the latter after he saw company representatives at a triathlon. Later, he wrote to them and they agreed to supply him with all the popsicles he wanted. He's hoping as the company grows, the partnership may lead to financial support. But Dan is grateful even for smaller sponsorships and is proud to wear their stuff or mention their name when he speaks.

While some of Dan's sponsorships involve a signed contract, many deals are made with just a friendly handshake. Since looking for sponsors can take just as much time as training, over the years Dan has backed off on his letter-writing campaign and tries to just get by financially while focusing on his actual training.

Mono-skier Chris Waddell is one of the few athletes who has managed to make ski racing and related activities his full-time occupation. When he's not skiing, training, or competing in summer wheelchair events, he works as a consultant for the Olympic Committee on Paralympic issues and offers instructional camps for aspiring mono-skiers along with teammate Sarah Will. Since 1994, Chris has been sponsored by The Hartford Financial Services Group for whom he does a variety of speaking engagements at schools and hospitals, and for sales people and clients. He also participates in Time-Warner Cable's "Cable in the Classroom" program, speaking to schools that have won awards for the best use of cable as an educational tool. Chris credits some of his good fortune to knowing a lot of people, but because people are unaware of the USDST, he admits getting sponsors is difficult. Chris believes "cold calling" or sending out information hasn't worked very well for most athletes because of the extra educational step required by disabled athletes. Before a company is willing to sponsor an athlete, needs to be educated about disabled skiing and the benefits of working with a world class athlete—one who just happens to be a disabled world class athlete.

Despite his success in obtaining sponsors, even Chris views funding as a huge and never-ending challenge and agrees sponsorship of the Team is generally lacking. He greatly appreciates Ski TAM, an annual benefit put on by the cable and telecommunications industry, both for their personal and financial support of the Team. Ski TAM takes place in Vail Colorado each spring at the end of the competition season. The four-day event, which began in 1995 with 150 participants from 12 sponsoring organizations, attracted 700 participants from 60 sponsors in 2001 and raised $400,000. Industry executives, personnel, and their guests enjoy two days of race clinics, dining, and dancing at local establishments with Team members, and outdoor adventures such as tubing at a local hill. On Saturday, teams consisting of one USDST member and four company representatives compete for gold, silver, and bronze medals in a slalom course. A reception, banquet, and silent auction conclude the day, along with awards presentations and a showing of videos from the day's racing. Ski TAM allows sponsors to build relationships with the athletes, both on and off the slopes, and gives the Team members an opportunity to show their appreciation. In addition to providing much-needed funds, the industry members have also become some of the Team's biggest fans.

One of the best educational tools to assist athletes in obtaining funding is getting potential sponsors to watch a race. Once people view the Team's athletic abilities, they understand the exciting competition involved with the sport. Team members agree that once someone sees a racing event, they really want to become involved.

Chapter 12
The Sweet Taste of Victory

When Sarah Will arrived at the 1992 Paralympics in Tignes, France, she knew she was ready to race. She had trained all summer on her own, lifting weights, taking long treks on her chair, and participating in road races. Because she was physically prepared, she was also more mentally prepared than she had ever been. She'd also gone to a certified Rolfer to cleanse her body of toxins and increase flexibility. Standing at the top of the downhill racecourse, she'd never felt better. Her goal was not to do her personal best; it was to be the best skier in the world.

As soon as she flew out of the starting gate, Sarah knew that she was going to take the race to the finish line. As she raced, the adrenalin rushed through her body and her lips and hands became completely numb. Throughout the race, she set herself up exactly where she wanted to be for the next section. As she came to the last pitch, she reached 60 miles per hour—the fastest she'd ever gone on a mono-ski—and felt terrified. She crossed the finish line knowing she was safe at the bottom, and that it was the best run of her life.

When Sarah turned around to look at the scoreboard, her thoughts were confirmed. She was in first place. All of her training and preparation had paid off, and it became the highlight of her career. Later, as Sarah sat proudly on the podium to receive her medal for herself and her country, she felt a sense of accomplishment that comes only from doing one's best. She vowed that someday she would give back that incredible feeling of accomplishment to others, and she knew she would succeed, for now she knew what she was capable of.

Two years later at the Lillehammer Paralympics, mono-skier Chris Waddell had the same goal in mind as Sarah—he wanted to be the fastest mono-skier in the world, regardless of class. Chris had already won his first Paralympic gold at the Albertville Winter Games. But to achieve his new goal, he had to overcome his biggest challenge—fear. Setting his goals, training hard, and preparing for years paid off, as they had for Sarah. He won the downhill gold and became the world's fastest mono-skier.

While being the fastest disabled skier was a goal for Sarah and Chris, other Team members point to other highlights of their careers, like placing in the top 10 in the Paralympics or winning the coveted World Cup overall—signifying they have consistently skied well throughout World Cup season. For amputee Dan Kosick making the Team still stands out as the highlight of his career. For Dan and others, living the dream of training, competing, and traveling with some of the best ski racers in the world is a victory in and of itself. Anyone who makes the Team can be considered a winner.

Others set their first goals on beating a team member in their class. For amputee Monte Meier, the 1994 Lillehammer Games stand out as the first highlight of his career. The day of the men's slalom, he awoke to bitter cold, which reminded him of winters back in Minnesota where nostrils stick together from the freezing moisture. But since he'd grown up skiing on such hard snow, he felt comfortable with the conditions, and he knew his ski was sharp enough to hold an edge. So later, when Monte flew out of the starting gate and navigated the slalom course, he gave it everything he had and surprised himself by coming in third place. Monte felt a thrill receiving the bronze medal at the awards ceremony alongside teammate Greg Mannino, who had won the silver. But hearing the German national anthem being played for gold medalist Alexander Spitz, who had been competing neck and neck with Greg for years, didn't seem right to Monte. He vowed he would fix that problem in the next Paralympics.

The Lillehammer Games also became pivotal for teammate Chris Devlin-Young. On the first day in Norway, during a warm-up run for the downhill, Chris's ski popped off when he stopped at the bottom of the hill, sending him crashing into the snow. Because he didn't have sensation in his legs, Chris couldn't feel that he had cracked the top of his shinbone and stretched the cartilage in his knee. For the next several days Chris sat on the sidelines watching his teammates compete in the event he had spent the last 10 years training for. In hopes that the swelling would go down and Chris could race in the other events, every evening the doctors drained blood and fluid from his knee. Chris wasn't just hoping he could ski at the Paralympics, he knew perfectly well he was going to, even though he knew it would be the last stand-up race of his life. A week and a half later, just in time for the super G, Chris was back on the slopes. Amazingly, he placed sixth in the super G and fourth in the giant slalom.

For the final race, the slalom, Chris was moved to a different disability class, since not enough racers had shown up to fill his class. Racing against people with less disability put Chris at a slight disadvantage, and slalom was already his worst event since he was more of a speed skier. Still, Chris had his sights set on medalling.

The day of the race the temperature dropped twenty degrees, and the icy slope left over from watering down the Olympic courses was icier than Chris had ever skied. Chris had never before heard his name called out during a race, but halfway down the slalom, he heard his name through the loudspeaker. Although it momentarily distracted him, Chris pulled his focus back onto his skiing. As he crossed the finish line, cheers rang out from the crowd. He'd gotten his gold. Later, at the awards ceremony, Chris wept openly as he saw the American flag rise above the crowd. Once again he had a chance to serve his country. This time instead of saving lives, he'd done it by winning gold.

Some Team members set their sights on beating a teammate as the first sign of victory. When Jason Lalla made the C Team, he was determined to beat Monte, who was already both a Paralympic and World Championship medalist. Jason entered the 1998 Columbia Crest Cup in Winter Park with that thought in mind. That year, the Columbia Crest Cup would help decide which of the five LW2's would be allowed to race in each event at the upcoming Paralympic Games in Nagano Japan. Of the five, Greg and Monte were already established as the top two A/K amputees. That left Matt Perkins, Dan, and Jason to battle for the third spot. In training races, Jason had been edging out Dan and Matt in just about every event except slalom. Jason knew that while the Team members had been working together and pushing each other to become better skiers during training, skiing would once again became an individual sport when they got to the race start.

At the Columbia Crest Cup, Jason surpassed his expectations, beating Monte three races in a row and earning two overall second-place finishes. He'd accomplished his first goal, which boosted his confidence, and set his sights on the Paralympics.

When the Team arrived in Nagano for the 1998 Paralympic Games, no one expected the welcome they received. Monte expected the Games would be a little bigger than the other disabled races he'd been to where a hundred or so people would show up, but he couldn't believe the crowds in Nagano. On race days, the grandstands were packed, and people lined both sides of the racecourse, sometimes five deep. Some of the spectators had little campfires alongside the run and rang bells as athletes came down the course. Others held up banners to encourage their favorites. Realizing that those people had come to watch disabled athletes race was, Monte says, "exciting and awesome."

It wasn't only on the hill that racers felt welcome. In Japan, being a ski racer was like being a celebrity. Since the Japanese papers had listed all of their profiles, people knew them by name. Whenever members of the Team left the Olympic village to go roam around town, they were surrounded by children and teens wanting to take pictures and asking for their autographs—and not just on paper. Many wanted to have their $400 ski jackets autographed with a permanent marker.

Two weeks before Nagano, at her first international race, Muffy Davis had won three World Cups—a giant slalom, a downhill and a super G. As a relative newcomer, she had wanted to go to Japan being the unknown and come out winning. But when Muffy got to Japan, she realized she'd peaked two weeks early. Like many of her teammates, Muffy had never skied on the kind of ice she encountered there. Between that and the mental pressure that came with competing in the Paralympics, instead of medalling, Muffy fell in her first three events. The hardest thing in the world for Muffy to do was to get back up on the mountain. She didn't want to fall again.

Knowing she was suffering from performance anxiety, Muffy let go of the pressure she was putting on herself and reset her goals for the remaining slalom race. Although slalom was her worst event, she remembered why she was racing—to do her best. Instead of trying to medal, Muffy focused on having fun, skiing her best, and finishing two clean runs. Whether she came in fifth or sixth didn't matter. Her new goal was simply to cross the finish line. Her attitude worked; Muffy placed third, winning her first Paralympic medal.

For Dan Kosick, the Nagano Paralympics were the first international races of his career. He arrived in Japan feeling like a little guy, but left feeling much differently. He and teammate Matt Perkins were the Team's rookies and had heard scary stories about the great European skiers, the numbers of competitors, and how intimidating international competition can be. Since each country was allowed to enter only three athletes per race, Dan would just race the speed events—downhill and super G. Dan took fourth in the downhill, barely missing third. But despite missing the bronze, Dan was pleased with his performance. After all, when a skier places fourth at the Paralympics, he is fourth in the world and that in itself is a great accomplishment. Before Nagano, no one even knew his name.

The day after the race, people came up to him, recognizing him for his abilities. Dan could sit back, enjoy his accomplishment, and cheer on his teammates Jason, Monte, and Greg, who would soon be competing in the technical events—giant slalom and slalom.

In the super G, Jason gracefully navigated the top of the course, but halfway down, in a completely flat spot, his boot dragged in the snow, and his ski came out from underneath him, sending him crashing into the snow. He quickly got up and kept going and, despite the fall, ended up 14th out of a field of over 80 skiers. Jason couldn't help but feel disappointed, knowing that if he hadn't crashed, his standing would be much higher. But Jason knew that two days later he'd have another chance to prove himself, this time in the giant slalom.

For Jason, the pressure was on. This event was what he'd spent years training for. Jason's parents and aunt had flown the 7,000 miles to watch, and were among the over 20,000 spectators who had shown up to watch the events. To ease the pressure, on the day of the giant slalom, Jason didn't speak to anyone. In fact, he hardly looked at anybody. He just focused on what he had to do. Knowing the giant slalom was one of his best events, he figured if he skied up to his potential, he stood a decent chance of medalling.

Jason pushed out of the starting gate and all the months of training and preparation kicked in, taking him downhill automatically. He skied a solid run, came through the last gate, and dropped into a tuck for the finish. But the thick slushy March snow at the bottom of the run caught him off guard and he bobbled, fighting to retain control. He reached out with one of his outriggers to catch himself and glided through the finish. Certain he'd blown the race, he looked up at the scoreboard as he heard cheers and screams from the people in the finish area. To his surprise, his run had placed him second. Jason's excitement grew as he realized he would probably stay in second for the run, since all the other top racers had already skied. If he could have another run like this one, but without the bobble at the end, he had a shot at the gold.

Before the second race, Jason used the same strategy, keeping to himself until it was time to race. This time he put in a clean run, crossed the finish, and looked up at the scoreboard. He quickly read through the top five names and hung his head when he didn't see his own. Then he looked up and saw his teammates Monte and Greg going nuts, screaming. Jason looked again at the scoreboard. There was his name in first place.

Monte was right behind him by a couple hundredths of a second, with Greg placing third. Jason felt ecstatic realizing only one remaining racer had a chance to beat him. That meant he'd at least won the silver.

The teammates waited in anticipation as the racer who was in first place after the first run came down, crossed the finish line, and placed fourth. The U.S. Team swept the event, taking the gold, silver, and bronze. For Jason, standing on the podium later alongside his friends as three American flags were raised and the national anthem played felt surreal. Jason's first Paralympic Games made him a champion.

When Monte arrived in Nagano, he felt strong and prepared. He was pleased with his silver medal in the giant slalom but still remembered his pledge at the last Paralympics that the American national anthem would play when he was on the podium. After the first slalom run, he was in first place by a second. Being that far ahead made him nervous, for to lose a lead that big would be a huge blow. To calm himself, he went off free skiing alone while the rest of the racers finished the course. Monte nearly got lost and arrived back at the starting gate just in time for the coaches to click him into his racing ski, enter the starting house, and push off for his second run. The seven years of training and determination to win a gold finally paid off as he out-skied Greg by a little over two seconds. He stood proudly on the podium to receive the gold medal he'd vowed to win four years before.

When George Sansonetis showed up in Nagano, as the only American LW9, he didn't know what to expect. Many of his teammates knew at least some of their competitors because they'd trained and raced alongside them all year. But this was George's first international race, and while the coaches all knew what he was up against, they didn't give any details. George just knew that the other guys were good. Feeling intimidated at first, George put aside his doubts, knowing that he needed to just focus on getting from the top to the bottom of the course as fast as he could without blowing out. He'd been training for this moment all year and knew he was in great shape. Still, he didn't know if he was good enough.

During his first downhill training run, George crashed. But on race day, he switched to a longer pair of skis and when he neared the bottom of the course, saw the last gate, and watched himself cross the finish line, even though he didn't medal George knew he was already a winner. He'd finished a race in Paralympic competition. His performance improved even more and in the super G, he won the bronze.

In preparation for the giant slalom, he and Ray Watkins skied an inspection run through the course—a typical routine for skiers before a race. Knowing both George's strengths and weakness, Ray told him what line he thought he should take and where he'd probably have the most difficulty. When they got to the bottom, Ray asked George what he thought of the course and proceeded to answer all of George's questions and concerns. During the second inspection run, Ray asked George to explain how he would ski through each of the gates and where he thought he should and shouldn't take chances. After George fully memorized the course, he felt more confident about the race.

George was the last one in his class to race in the giant slalom, and as he neared the last gate, he knew he'd skied a good run. When he came through the finish line, looked up, and saw his name on the scoreboard in the top three, tears welled up in his eyes as he felt a new energy surge through his body. After six years and $40,000, he'd finally achieved the dream he had since high school. He won his first medal, a silver. At the awards ceremony, George was speechless. Winning medals gave him a sense of accomplishment he'd never before experienced, and he felt happier than he had in his life, knowing he had accomplished his dreams and could do anything he set his mind to.

The women's team also had its share of victories at Nagano. Mary Ridell won the silver in the downhill but still had her sights set on a gold medal. The morning of the women's giant slalom, she awoke with the feeling she was going to win. Every muscle in her body was toned and programmed to race. She'd been dreaming of winning a Paralympic gold medal since early childhood, and now she had her chance. When she finished the run, Mary knew she was in first place, but one other skier still had to race—Ramona Hoh from Canada, who was in front by about a half second after the first run. Mary watched anxiously as the Canadian raced well through the upper portion of the course. Then she made a right turn, bobbled, and then pulled herself back in line. But Mary noticed the Canadian's drive wane, and from that point on Mary knew the race was hers.

Later, as she watched the American flag go up for her and heard the American national anthem, Mary thought about all the people who'd supported her in getting to that moment—her coaches, sponsors, family, friends, and teammates—and experienced the greatest feeling of her life. Not only had she finally achieved her long-held dream, she also knew that she could achieve whatever goals she set in the future. And while she got the bronze in the slalom, winning the gold still stands out as the highlight of her career.

The U.S. Team ended up winning a total of 32 medals at Nagano, including 13 golds. Three-tracker Sarah Billmeier medalled in all four events, winning gold in the downhill and slalom and taking bronze in the giant slalom and silver in the super G. B/K amputee Jennifer Kelchner won gold in the downhill. Sarah Will showed a strong performance, taking the gold in the slalom, giant slalom, and super G, and the silver in downhill. Greg won the gold in both downhill and super G and took the bronze in the giant slalom. Jake Rife had a solid performance, winning a silver in giant slalom and a bronze in the super G. Chris Waddell won gold in the downhill, silver in the slalom, and silver in the super G. The Team had kept its standing as the number-one disabled team in the world.

While Muffy Davis was happy to win the bronze in slalom at Nagano, her biggest career accomplishment would come later, during the 2000 - 2001 ski season, when she won the overall World Cup title. While winning a gold medal is only representative of one race on one day of a skier's life, winning the overall shows that a skier races consistently well. And winning the World Cup overall made Muffy the top woman mono-skier racer in the world. While she felt proud of her personal accomplishment, when she sat on the podium, she knew she was not alone. All the people who'd stood behind her were right there with her, her family, friends, and hometown who'd supported her all the years she dreamed of being an Olympian. And she knew one of the reasons for her success was that she'd shifted her focus. Instead of being competitive with everyone on her team and thinking there was only room for one of them to succeed, she had started helping out her teammates, knowing that helping them win helped her succeed. She now believes that anyone can have whatever they desire if he or she just helps enough other people get what they desire.

For amputee Clay Fox, the 2001 World Championships would become one of the most memorable events of his life. Since he was a B-teamer in the largest class, LW2, Clay almost didn't get chosen to accompany the Team to Europe. He remembered the first time he'd raced in Europe and only finished one race out of twelve because of the unfamiliar, icy conditions. But since then, he'd been training hard, so when the coaches selected him as one of the LW2s, he felt apprehensive but prepared.

Clay inspected the downhill course during the first training run, taking note of challenging turns and planning where he could find speed. But during the second downhill training run, he caught an edge and crashed through two fences lining the course. The next day in the downhill race, his sore knee and shoulder kept him from placing well. In fact, he skied very poorly. Discouraged, Clay tried to psych himself up for the super G. On the day of the race, Clay felt confident, and he ended up placing fifth. His teammates excitedly congratulated him, thinking as he did that because he didn't have a strong track record, fifth was probably the best he'd achieve. But soon Clay would discover his true potential.

The day of the giant slalom, Clay arose feeling "in the zone," that place an athlete can only enter after months of preparation and training. For the first time, Clay felt he was going to win. But by the time he skied his first run, the course was totally rutted. Most of the other more disabled classes—the mono-skiers, LW9's, three-trackers and blind skiers—had already raced first, as they always did. What's more, it had rained the night before, adding to the poor conditions. But despite the rutted course, Clay kept telling himself that he could win, and he skied a pretty decent first run in his usual "O.C. style" – that's the way his teammates labeled the out-of-control appearance he always exhibited skiing. Near the end, Clay almost missed the third-to-last gate, but quickly caught himself and worked his way around it. Discouraged, Clay figured he'd blown the race, but surprised himself by placing a tenth of second ahead of the second-place finisher. Knowing he had a chance to medal, Clay decided to really go for it in the second run. Racing down the course, Clay could feel the years of training kick in as he glided across the finish line—in first place by one and one-half seconds. The whole team, who were generally placing poorly at the Championships, exploded into cheers. Later, as Clay stood on the podium listening to the national anthem with his gold medal around his neck, having a disability was the furthest thing from his mind. He thought only of how good it felt to win for himself, his team, and his country. Sharing the excitement of his victory, Clay's teammates picked him up off the podium and carried him away.

After the World Championships, the Team traveled to Wilschönau, Austria for the World Cup Finals where Csilla Kristof got to taste her first international race medal. Standing in the starting gate for the GS, Csilla pumped herself up, waiting for the signal to push off. Once on the run, she concentrated on keeping her hand forward—something her coaches had been telling her all her life. She knew that by keeping focused on one aspect, the rest of her training would fall into place and she'd keep her aggressive edge. She skied a good run and during the last half of the course, she knew she was doing really well. As she crossed the finish line, she heard the cheers of the approving crowd, and won the silver. Although she'd previously won the gold in GS at the Nationals, for her, placing second among the world's best athletes brought her to the next level of racing.

Chapter 13
Benefits On and Off the Slopes

Anyone who enjoys skiing knows the pleasure that comes from being out in fresh mountain air, viewing the surrounding landscape from ski lifts and mountaintops, and the feeling of wind brushing across your face as you glide across the snow-covered hillside. Skiing also improves strength, endurance, and balance, which is especially beneficial for people with disabilities. Racers also experience the exciting rush of adrenalin that comes from skiing at high speeds, not to mention the thrill of standing on a podium receiving a hard-earned medal and achieving a lifelong dream. Members of the USDST have the opportunity to travel the world, meet people from different cultures, and make friendships that often last a lifetime. Mastering a sport and racing against—and sometimes beating— able-bodied peers give people with disabilities a new confidence that carries over into the rest of their lives. For members of the USDST, doors often open to new careers and opportunities that they may never have imagined before ski racing. While these benefits are all worthwhile, the ones disabled athletes mention most involve the places they've seen, the friends they've made, and the personal changes that come from working hard and being among other elite disabled athletes.

Skiing has been called by some the perfect sport for its accessibility to both able-bodied and disabled persons. Disabled skiers can be as good as if not better than able-bodied skiers and can recreationally or competitively ski the same runs and courses. Skiing has nothing to do with having one or two legs, being paralyzed or vision impaired. The sport brings people together, which is why Allison Jones originally began skiing after she lost her leg. Once again she could play alongside her family.

Many racers love the speed, thrill, and adrenalin rush that comes with racing, and some, like Adam Fromma, are admitted adrenalin junkies. As an outdoor lover, Adam also enjoys the fact that ski racing allows him to be in the mountains and loves the feeling of motion, an experience often harder to come by for people with disabilities. Basically, skiing puts him in a good mood.

While some benefits like an adrenalin rush are temporary, the personal growth gained from skiing and training with the USDST is a benefit that lasts a lifetime. Because coaches and teammates expect everyone to be self-sufficient, Team members learn to become very responsible. They are expected to carry their own ski equipment, including mono-skis and outriggers, wheel themselves to and from the slopes, and take care of the financial aspects of being a Team member.

Amputee Mary Ridell credits being a member of the USDST with building self-confidence, communication skills, and the ability to concentrate and stay focused on goals. Since she made the Team at age fourteen, she grew up with the members and considers them family. And she realizes she has a level of maturity and confidence she doesn't see in others her age.

"I'm twenty and I feel like I have a base for my life and know what I want. I know myself now," she says. "I know a lot of people who are twenty-five and twenty-six who really don't know themselves." And while she loves winning races, Mary says it's the friends she's made and the lessons she's learned that will last a lifetime.

Besides the opportunity to travel, meet interesting people and learn about different cultures, amputee Dan Kosick finds his whole level of self-confidence and outlook has shifted and says that being on the ski team has better prepared him to face everyday obstacles. "In everyday life, no matter what I'm doing [skiing] effects that and makes me a better person overall. Little things today might have been really big things to overcome before, but they're not so big anymore because I've seen so much."

Spinal-cord-injured Carl Burnett found that training and succeeding in a sport he is passionate about gave him a real sense of accomplishment. Although he attends Dartmouth College, Carl wanted something in his life besides college and settling into a traditional career. Attending college in the spring and summer and then training and racing with the Team in the fall and winter gives him the opportunity to live a kind of lifestyle a lot of people only dream about.

Most Team members cite the camaraderie and friendship that develop among teammates as some of the biggest benefits to being on the USDST, especially since it is often the first time they've had a chance to meet others who are well-adjusted to their disabilities. Growing up, many children with disabilities do not have any peers with whom they can share their circumstances and really be understood. When athletes first get involved with disabled ski racing, it can seem unnerving to be surrounded by so many people with disabilities, but in general it helps them gain self-confidence. Growing up, arm amputee Adam Fromma was the only disabled kid in school. He was the only disabled kid bowling, playing baseball, and skateboarding. When he made the Team, all of a sudden he was surrounded by people with disabilities and became comfortable hanging out with teammates, walking into an establishment and knowing everybody wasn't necessarily looking at him. "It definitely did good for my spirits," he says. And Adam enjoyed having other understanding ears to share funny stories like going through the metal detectors at airports with his prosthesis.

For Allison Pearl, being on the team has opened up a new awareness of disabilities. Since making the team, she's noticed that some days she even forgets she has a disability. Her experience has taught her that people with disabilities are normal. They just happen to be missing parts or have some parts that aren't working. Alison now views disabilities merely as little roadblocks that people find different ways around.

Jason Lalla claims he's met some of his best friends through ski racing, especially people with whom he feels a common bond. When he was first injured, Jason didn't want to be different. While at one level he didn't think he was, part of him acknowledged that his disability *did* make him different, and that led to some insecurities. When Jason saw that all the other amputees were completely comfortable with missing a leg or arm, he began to question why he felt so conflicted. Once he accepted his disability as normal, he noticed others doing the same. Hanging around with other Team members like Greg Mannino and Monte Meier and seeing their zest for life and positive attitudes totally shifted Jason's beliefs about being disabled. He found out he basically wasn't disabled. His only wish is that he had starting racing sooner rather than suffering for five years.

Amputee Dan Kosick also credits his self-confidence to being around confident athletes with disabilities. Before he made the Team, he was very hesitant going into public with one leg because he wasn't sure what other people would think of him. But once Dan got back into sports and saw other people doing well, he realized he was as good or better than a lot of people and stopped caring what others thought. "Skiing has definitely helped with attitude," he says.

George Sansonetis, who because of his dystonia skis better than he walks, notices that when he's skiing, he's not thinking about his disability or the way people look at him. When he was younger, he thought looks counted more than what's inside a person. Now he doesn't care if someone stares at him as he walks down the street with his distinctive involuntary movements. He says he now knows its what's inside that matters.

While being part of the Team helps many disabled skiers adjust to their disabilities, Chris Waddell has also found that being involved with sports opens up a comfortable arena for able-bodied people to ask and learn about disabilities. When he's wheeling down the street in his chair, it's not always appropriate or polite for people to ask questions about his disability or what happened. But sharing the ski slopes bridges the gap and gives both children and adults a comfortable ground to ask questions.

Traveling around the world is another of the biggest benefits to being on the USDST. It's winter wherever the Team goes, the trips involve long, hard hours of training and racing, and the lifestyle of living in a hotel can get old. But seeing new places, meeting interesting people, and learning about different cultures offer Team members experiences they'll treasure for the rest of their lives. For those who never traveled much in their youth, ski racing offers a first taste of new cultures. Prior to ski racing, Dan had never been outside of New York except for some small family vacations. And Chicago-native Sandy Dukat, who worked long intense hours before training to make the Team, found living in Colorado shifted her whole pace of life. She says she no longer drives like a maniac and that being in the mountains slowed down her state of mind. Many current team members have competed in Japan, Austria, Switzerland, and across the United States and Canada. Not only do they get to travel, they also get to represent their country. For amputee Clay Fox, that's one of the best parts of ski racing. And Chris Devlin-Young, whose life in a sense has been dedicated to his country, first by serving in the Coast Guard, now represents his country in the international race circuit.

Besides all the other benefits of being with the Team, members also gain valuable skills applicable to other areas of their lives and often discover previously unrealized career opportunities. Jason credits his years on the Team with not only allowing him to excel once again in a sport and help him adjust to his disability, but also with teaching him the value of hard work. During high school, he played sports and, in a sense, everything was given to him. He lived at home and didn't have to focus on anything but being a good athlete. But since being on the Team requires skiers to raise their own funds, Jason learned how to run a successful fundraising campaign and to deal with major corporations on a professional level. As blind skier Andy Parr says, if a skier can keep organized, raise funds, stay fit, and produce good results on the hill, that can help him transcend anything in the future.

For some racers, racing has already opened up new career opportunities. Mono-skier Sarah Will has been on national television advertisements for Chevy Trucks and interviewed athletes for an Internet site called Access Life. And teammate Chris Waddell, who does speaking engagements for his sponsor, The Hartford Services Group, has been featured in *Outside* and *People* magazines and on *60 Minutes, The Oprah Winfrey Show, Dateline*, and ESPN. He even landed a role in a soap opera. Amputee Greg Mannino has already gained experience working in the prosthetics and orthotics industry.

After retirement, the experience of being a Team member may also open up other career opportunities in the ski industry, like positions as an equipment representative, coach, or ski instructor. As head coach Ewald Zirbisegger says, when Team members retire, they will be recognized for their abilities, not their disability, in whatever avenues they pursue.

While mono-skier Muffy Davis likes to think that the personal growth she's experienced in recent years is partly from an increase in maturity as she gets older, she also credits her experiences on the USDST. Although she loves winning medals, the best part for Muffy is that in America, being a medalist gives a person credibility to inspire others, which is Muffy's true passion. Through her experiences as a competitive ski racer, Muffy has also learned that there's room enough in the world for everyone to succeed. In fact, when she decided to help others on the Team achieve their goals, she found it was easier to achieve her own. In looking back over the years since her injury, Muffy feels the challenges she's faced have made her the person she is today. In her experience, disability doesn't change a person. Instead, being paralyzed opened her up to her true soul and spirit. She learned the depths of her strength and found what she is capable of. And succeeding on the Team, Muffy now knows that she can handle anything that is put before her. If Muffy could take a magic pill and walk tomorrow, she'd definitely do it. But if it meant giving up the past twelve years and changing who she has become, she wouldn't. She has no regrets. The journey has ultimately been rewarding and fulfilling.

Muffy is not the only one who feels their life is better because of the opportunities that stemmed from having a disability. Although Greg wouldn't wish an injury like his on anyone, he says because of his injury and being part of the ski team, he's become a better person. "I've had a successful, fantastic career," he says. "I've gone everywhere. I never would have had that opportunity if this didn't happen."

In addition to the many medals he's won in disabled competitions, Greg has competed against some of the top able-bodied racers in the world and become friends with many of them. And Greg is respected for his athleticism and who he is, not because he's disabled. Being with the Team so many years, Greg has also reaped the benefit of seeing younger Team members grow up from little kids into young men and women who achieve their own goals. And, Greg says, the sport keeps him young.

For Chris Devlin-Young, racing gave him back mastery over his body and lifted the depression that set in when he became disabled. Skiing also gave him back a sense of freedom and gave him some direction. Chris realizes that since becoming involved with racing, he lives a better lifestyle overall than before his injury, admitting that some parts are worse and some parts better, like the fact that he met his wife through teammate Chris Waddell.

After all the hard work and hours of training, when racers finally taste the sense of accomplishment that comes from winning a medal, they usually describe it as one of the greatest feelings of their lives. But the real win comes from knowing that whatever goals they set for themselves in the future will be achievable. They've learned how to do whatever it takes to accomplish their future dreams.

Chapter 14
Future Goals and Dreams

Through the experiences involved in preparing to become a ski racer, making the Team, and training and competing nationally and internationally, members of the USDST gain valuable skills they will continue to use throughout their lives. Some of the skills they use repeatedly both on and off the slopes are the ability to set goals, develop a plan of action, and achieve those goals. Several disabled ski racers already have their sights set on new goals after they retire from the Team. For some that involves giving back to the sport that enriched their life. Others plan on finishing college or using the degrees they already have in other career pursuits. And still others plan on continuing to race in the foreseeable future.

After the 2002 Paralympic Games in Salt Lake City, many athletes plan on retiring from the Team. Kevin Bramble plans on becoming a civil engineer after finishing his studies at the University of Nevada. Muffy Davis, who always knew skiing was just going to be one part of her life, plans on giving back some of what she's learned through motivational speaking, hoping her experiences and challenges will encourage and inspire others. Another of Muffy's goals is to break down the stereotypes towards people with disabilities by hosting a talk show from her wheelchair about amazing people as a forum to speak openly about disabilities. Muffy believes disability will eventually affect everyone if they live long enough and refers to able-bodied people as TABs— temporarily able-bodied.

Some team members plan on continuing to race following the 2002 Paralympics. Csilla Kristof, who's finishing up her senior year at Burke Mountain Academy, hopes to stay on the Team until after the 2006 Paralympics. Then, she says, she definitely wants to go to college. The question on her mind is whether to turn her focus towards school, skiing, or try to do both like some members of the Team. Mary Riddell, who considers ski racing her career, plans to continue racing until she's reached her personal best. Her sights are not just set on competing against disabled athletes. Mary also foresees competing in more able-bodied races—and winning. Her ultimate ski goal is to be in the top echelon of able-bodied racers at the FIS level. If she surpasses that goal, she says she'll move on from there. Since Mary describes herself as the type of person who puts all her efforts into one endeavor, she says she won't move onto other things, like devoting herself to going to school or creating a successful marriage, until she feels the sense of accomplishment from skiing her best.

Other athletes who plan to continue racing after the Paralympics have their sights set on careers following racing. Jason Lalla plans on staying with work that's familiar rather than learning a totally new trade from the ground up. Since he remains passionate about skiing, that means either finding a job in the ski industry or using the experience he gained in the field of prosthetics during a summer job as a technician for one of his sponsors, RGB prosthetics in San Diego. Even if Jason chooses the latter, he hopes to stay in the athletic side of things rather than focusing on geriatrics, which composes much of the industry. Monte Meier, who holds a bachelor's degree in finance from Metropolitan State University in St. Paul, Minnesota and a two-year degree in prosthetics from Century College in White Bear, Minnesota, plans either to get his brokerage license or go into real estate. Clay Fox plans to finish his degree in finance at the University of Wyoming. Andy Parr, who like many Team members has devoted the past several years to skiing, working odd jobs to support racing, plans to get a "real job" and make some money.

Lacey Heward, who hopes to continue racing until at least after the 2006 Paralympic Games, would eventually like to become a motivational speaker. In fact, that's one reason she pursued ski racing. Through her racing career, she hopes to gain inspirational stories and add credibility to her speaking skills. Sandy Dukat, who just made the team at the end of the 2000 - 2001 ski season, plans on devoting her time to ski racing for the foreseeable future. After that, she thinks she'd like to have her own outdoors program working with children, but foresees many possibilities after ski racing. Alison Pearl, who made the team along with Sandy, plans to go through the residency match program during the 2001 - 2002 school year and use her medical degree to go into radiology. But, she says, she's open to skiing taking priority for a while.

Some Team members plan on staying in the ski industry even after they retire from the team. Dan Kosick, who is undecided about whether to continue racing or retire following the 2002 Paralympics, hopes eventually to coach at Greek Peak Ski Area, the small mountain near his hometown where his skiing career began. Dan also plans to focus on other meaningful things in life like relationships, wanting to make sure he doesn't forget about the other important things in life besides skiing. Sarah Will already gives back to the sport through a ski camp she runs at Vail every winter with Chris Waddell. She sees a responsibility to helping the sport develop and become both faster and safer. Sarah would also like to help build other disabled people's confidence so they can become more comfortable with themselves. While she believes skiing will always be a part of her life, Sarah's future goals include simply living a happy life and raising a good family.

Chris Devlin-Young is another Team member who has already given back to the sport that gave him back, as he says, "the wind in his hair." Since he first learned to ski at the Disabled Veterans Winter Sports Clinic, he's been returning to the clinic each year as an instructor—except for the year that he needed to relearn disabled skiing as a mono-skier. Chris works as the head coach for the New England Disabled Ski Team, a racing program at Loon Mountain that he created shortly after relocating to the East Coast. Chris is also committed to expanding possibilities for disabled skiers beyond racing. He has already expanded the horizons for disabled skiers by competing in the National Extreme Championships in both the alpine and snowboard categories, the latter on a mono-snowboard that he designed. He also competed in the World Synchronized Ski Championships and was the first to bring a team of disabled skiers to the event. Through his example, he hopes disabled skiers will learn that many opportunities exist for disabled skiers besides ski racing.

Adam Fromma, who plans on taking a year off after the Paralympic Games, is thinking about going back to school, perhaps on the East Coast, and exploring avenues besides skiing. But Adam doesn't foresee ever giving up the sport that has so greatly enriched his life. "Even when my career is over as far as ski racing goes, I will still be on the mountain," he says. "Whether I'm back instructing at Jiminy [Peak, in Massachusetts] or whether I'm here [in Colorado], I'll still definitely be out there." After all, he says, "It's been a great ride."

Chapter 15
The Future of Disabled Ski Racing

Since its origin in the early 1970's, disabled ski racing has evolved from a "weekend warrior" sport based on a medical rehabilitation model to a group of elite athletes with a year-round commitment to training and racing. Many more options now exist for disabled skiers to compete at the local, national, and international level than ever before. Following the trend of recent years toward increased competition, the Team plans on continuing to train hard to retain its position as the number-one disabled ski team in the world. But with many Team members planning on retiring after the 2002 Paralympic Games in Salt Lake City, the Team faces ongoing challenges to retain that status.

One of the biggest challenges the Team faces is filling its future ranks to keep its dominance. With that in mind, DS/USA has been busy developing a stronger feeder program with more level 1 and 2 races around the country. Former Team manager Steve Stone would also like to see more of the athletes going to rehab hospitals to educate people about their experiences with disability and what they've accomplished through skiing. While this type of program was popular during the Vietnam era, in more recent years, outreach programs have not been as prevalent. With increased competition from Austria, Germany, Switzerland, Canada, and Japan, the need to educate people with disabilities about the opportunities available through ski racing will remain a number one priority for the Team.

One advantage disabled skiers have is that one need not begin racing at an early age to make the Team. Despite the increased competitiveness, disabled racing remains a sport that people can begin pursuing in late adolescence or even in their twenties. As Jack Benedick points out, the Team is not composed just of people who were elite athletes before they got injured. Even today, any disabled person could potentially train and get good enough to make the Team. And Team members welcome more disabled skiers becoming involved with racing. More racers means more competition, and everyone agrees that's a good thing. Winning a medal while competing against a field of 40 racers in an international competition brings a much greater sense of accomplishment than beating five contenders in a national race.

In addition to the need to fill the ranks of retiring athletes, the Team continues to face another big challenge—the difficulty of increasing public awareness. Many people remain unaware of the abilities of the Disabled Team, and often confuse the Paralympics with the Special Olympics— races for people with mental retardation and closely related developmental disabilities. While the Special Olympics provide an important sports venue for that population, they do not involve the level of athleticism required of USDST members. Even when people are aware of the differences between the Paralympics and the Special Olympics, most of the general public has no concept of the abilities of the disabled elite athlete. Jason Lalla feels the opinion of the general public is that disabled skiing is not as competitive as able-bodied skiing. While Jason admits this may be true outside the top level, he is quick to point out that competition among the top 5 percent of the athletes is as intense as any competition between the world's top able-bodied skiers.

Team members would like the public to respect the disabled athletes for their abilities, rather than just experiencing the heart warming feelings athletes often hear expressed. While the athletes realize people have good intentions, they would like more people to become aware that the USDST is composed of hard core athletes, not just inspirational people with disabilities. "Yes, we have less [of our body working than] regular able-bodied people have," Andy Parr says, "but we're still just as competitive, and we can probably out-rip most people on the lift." While some people are becoming aware of the abilities of the disabled population, it's a slow-moving process because, as Andy says, "sometimes people do judge a book by its cover."

Another ongoing challenge for the Team is obtaining funding. Even though some of the disabled athletes are multiple-Paralympic medalists and may have been ranked the best in the world for over 70 percent of their careers, corporate sponsorship remains lacking. Without the sponsorship that able-bodied skiers receive, disabled athletes find it difficult to juggle working and fundraising with the year-round training required to remain competitive. The result is that some good athletes drop out, which reduces the field of top competitors. Jason Lalla believes that once corporations start backing individual athletes, the sport will become more competitive because there will be more incentive to stay in the sport and athletes will be able to put 100 percent of their effort into skiing. Dan

Kosick agrees and hopes that in the future, more disabled athletes will make a good living as ski racers.

The Team would also like to see more spectators at local and national events, which up until now have been attended mostly by school children. Every Team member who raced in Nagano talks about the thrill of racing in front of a large crowd. But Team members do appreciate the younger fans and recognize the opportunity to help promote the sport.

"Children are the best people to see what you do," says Dan Kosick, "because they'll speak their mind. They'll go home and tell their dads and moms about what they saw and how amazing it is." And, Dan adds, children love to ask questions. "They'll ask the questions, and they'll grow up not being ignorant about disabilities."

Despite the challenges, strides toward increased public recognition are present across the country. In 1999, The New England Ski Museum hosted a special exhibit on disabled skiing, and in 1995, the National Sports Center for the Disabled and the Winter Park Recreational Association joined forces to establish the National Disabled Ski Hall of Fame. The hall, located atop Winter Park ski area, features a history of disabled skiing along with photos and biographies of Hall of Fame inductees. Inductees are honored for their contributions to skiing for people with disabilities, in either recreation or competition. As of 2000, thirteen skiers had been inducted including Hal O'Leary, founder of the National Sports Center for the Disabled; Vietnam veteran Doug Pringle who was a three-time national slalom champion and founder of what has become Disabled Sports USA; and amputee Diana Golden, who dominated the sport of disabled skiing for more than six years and was the first disabled skier to compete regularly in non-disabled events.

Another obstacle sometimes facing disabled skiers is accessiblity at ski areas. While many ski areas are already user-friendly for people with disabilities, a movement is underway to require every ski area to have accessible lifts and rest rooms. Peter Axelson is one of the pioneers in this movement, which would require that every chair lift be the correct height for self-loading mono-skis and that wheelchairs be available on the mountain to allow mono-skiers to use public restrooms and dining facilities at mid-mountain and mountain-top locations.

Chris Devlin-Young acknowledges all the advances that have occurred during his ski career to enable disabled skiers to be independent. Due to advances in mono-ski technology and accessibility, at many ski areas he can get from the parking lot to the snow, up the lifts, and down the trails without the need for any assistance. And advances in equipment mean he can carve some of the best turns of any skier—able-bodied or disabled.

With increased accessiblity at all ski areas, more level 1 and 2 races, more development camps, increased public awareness, and more corporate sponsorship, the USDST will remain the top contender in the world of disabled ski racing. It will continue to strive toward its goal of making disabled ski racing as much like the able-bodied version of the sport as possible. And with increased awareness and accessiblity, more people with disabilities will have the opportunity to discover the pleasures and benefits available from ski racing.

Appendices

Appendix A
Abbreviations

AFO – ankle-foot orthosis

A/K Amputee – above-the-knee amputee

B/K Amputee – below-the-knee amputee

CAF – Challenged Athletes Foundation

DS/USA – Disabled Sports USA

FIS – Federation Internationale de Ski (International Ski Federation)

GS – giant slalom

NSCD – National Sports Center for the Disabled

PSIA - The Professional Ski Instructors Association of America

SCI – spinal cord injury

USDST – United States Disabled Ski Team

USSA – United States Ski and Snowboard Association

difference in skiing between himself and able-bodied skiers. When he first began skiing, Adam played with various options, like holding a pole with the hook of his prosthesis, but decided to just ski without the pole or the hook attachment for his prosthesis.

In some ways, Adam feels fortunate to have a disability. To make the able-bodied national ski team, a racer must start training when he or she is young, and even then the competition is fierce. As a disabled skier, he only began racing when he was twenty-one and made the Team within five years, admitting that during those years he devoted himself to training and working hard. When Adam's not on the ski slopes, he's on his mountain bike or out camping or hiking. He has also taken up golf, and while he finds it a tough sport, he's getting better at it, and likely won't quit until he's mastered the sport.

Teammate Csilla Kristof grew up in Mammoth Lakes, California, naturally doing what just about everyone else did in town—learning to ski race. By the age of three, she was on skis, and she began racing when she was nine, joining the Mammoth Mountain Ski Team along with her classmates. Although she was born a left forearm amputee, she knew nothing of disabled ski programs and has always skied without a prosthesis.

One day when she was eleven, a coach spotted Csilla on the slopes and called out to her to stop. At first Csilla thought she must be in trouble, but soon learned that coach Chris Griffin, who was running a ski training camp that week, wanted her to meet the Team in the parking lot at the end of the day. When she did, Chris passed along his phone number and invited her to their upcoming camp in Breckenridge.

During the next three years, Csilla went to a few races, including the Ski Spectacular and the Huntsman Cup, while continuing to train at her home mountain. By age fourteen, she made the Team, becoming one of its youngest members ever. While Csilla was known to goof around with her friends on the slopes at Mammoth, she became more serious about racing and training once she made the Team. She set new goals for herself—like medalling in the 2002 Paralympics—and learned what it takes to win. To improve her racing skills, she enrolled in Burke Mountain Academy, a school on the East Coast geared toward ski racing, where she has the opportunity to train among able-bodied racers in addition to her camps with the Disabled Team.

Appendix B
Glossary

Ankle-foot orthosis (AFO) – A brace used to support the ankle and foot.

Amputee – A person with an amputated limb. According to a 2000 report by the Amputee Limb Loss Research and Statistics Program, 35 percent of all reported amputations were of the upper limb while 65 percent were of the lower limb.

    Upper-extremity amputation – Amputation of the arm. This disability can cause lateral balance problems. Skiers can ski with or without a prosthesis.

    Lower-extremity amputation – Amputation of the leg, classified by the level of loss. The largest percentage of limb amputations reported in 2000 were below-the knee (48%) while only 5 percent were-above-the knee.

    Below-the-knee amputation (B/K) – Skiers often ski with a specially designed sports prosthesis with a forward lean built into the ankle, using a suspension system to improve contact and keep the prosthesis firmly in place.

    Above-the-knee amputation. (A/K) – Skiers three-track with a single ski and two outriggers. In 2000, the most common causes of A/K amputation were trauma (34%), dysvascular disease without mention of diabetes (16%), diabetes (14%), cancer (8%), congenital (7%) and other (6%).

Bi-ski – A sit-down ski with two specially designed skis. Bi-skis are most commonly used by people lacking the upper body and trunk strength required to use a mono-ski. Bi-skiers usually ski with the assistance of a guide who skis behind them holding a tether to keep them under control.

Blind – Visually impaired. Blind skiers are classified into three categories, B1, B2, and B3, based upon their degree of vision loss. (See Appendix F)

Bucket – The seat portion of a mono-, bi-, or dual-ski.

Cant – A plastic wedge placed under the inside or outside edge of a ski boot to help ensure flat contact between the ski and the snow when running on flat terrain.

Congenital – Existing at birth. May be either hereditary or due to some influence during pregnancy, even up to the moment of birth.

Dual-ski – A sit-down ski with two normal skis. The dual-ski allows both skis to edge independently and has a similar frame design and shock absorber system to a mono-ski.

Dystonia – Abnormal tension of muscles.

Forearm crutches – A crutch consisting of a shaft extending from the ground to halfway between the wrist and elbow, with a horizontal handle and either a cuff or curved plastic piece that supports the user's forearm. Also known as Lofstrand or Canadian crutches.

Line – The path racers take through the gates.

Mono-ski – A sit-down ski composed of a metal frame supporting a molded seat or "bucket" suspended by a shock absorber mounted on a single ski.

Outriggers – A form of ski pole consisting of forearm crutches and ski tips used by sit-down skiers, three-trackers, and four-trackers for added stability and maneuverability.

Paresis – Partial paralysis, weakness of muscles.

Paralysis – Loss of power of voluntary movement in a muscle through injury or disease of its nerve supply.

Prosthesis – A fabricated substitute for a missing part of the body, such as an arm, foot, or leg.

Roller – A bump in the ski terrain. Also sometimes called a roll.

Sit-ski – A toboggan-like ski for sit-down skiers who choose to ski closer to the ground or those with injuries that do not allow them to use a mono-ski. Also used as a synonym for mono-ski, especially in Canada and Europe.

Spina bifida – A congenital disorder effecting the spinal cord with resulting weakness and paralysis.

Spinal cord injury (SCI) – Injury to the spinal cord often results in the disruption of voluntary movement and sensation below the level of injury. Often the result of a broken back, motor vehicle accidents are the most common cause of SCI (44%) followed by violence, primarily gunshot wounds (24%), falls (22%), recreational sporting activities (8%), and other causes including stab wounds and medical or surgical complications (2%). Two-thirds of the sports-related injuries are from diving. Snow skiing accounts for only 0.26% of the injuries.

Males represent 82 percent of SCI's, females 18 percent. Most SCI's (55%) occur between the ages of 16 and 30 years. Five percent occur between the ages of 1 and 14 years, 20 percent between 30 and 44 years, 10 percent between 45 and 59 years, and 10 percent in those over the age of 60.

Tether – A rope attached to the back of a sit-, mono-, bi, or dual-ski to guide or assist the skier down the hill.

Wedge – Made of dense foam, compact cardboard, or wood and placed inside or outside the skier's boot to help accommodate any lack of bend in the skier's ankle or prosthetic limb. Also used for seating in mono- bi- sit- and dual-skis.

Appendix C
Special Concerns for Skiers with Spinal Cord Injury

Since the spinal cord is made up of bundles of nerve fibers responsible for sending messages between the brain and muscles, injury to the cord most often results in partial (paresis) or complete loss of sensation and voluntary movement of muscles below the level of injury (paralysis).

People with SCI's must be careful to avoid hypothermia and skin irritation. If their injury is above mid-thoracic (T8), impairment in internal temperature control requires extra attention to dressing appropriately for cold temperatures. Skin sores can be avoided by shifting weight every few minutes. The most common areas for sores to develop are where bones are closest to the skin including ankles, knees, hips, sacrum, and sit bones (ischia). Involuntary movements of the muscles below the level of injury (spasticity) can often be relieved by repositioning the leg to ease the stretch on affected muscles. Loss of bladder control necessitates intermittent catheterization or the use of an indwelling catheter with a bag to collect urine, which must be drained when full. For SCI's with injuries above mid-thoracic (T6), a hypertensive crisis called autonomic dysreflexia may cause severe sweating, goose bumps, flushed feelings, chilling without fever, severe pounding headache, and increased spasticity, often the result of catheter irritation, skin pressure sores or spasticity from a stretched muscle.

Following is a generalized summary of losses experienced with different levels of SCI.

L4-5, S-1 – Loss of sensation at the level of injury, paralysis/paresis of hip extensors, knee flexors, and ankle flexors and extensors. Persons affected at this level usually can walk with the help of ankle-foot bracing and forearm crutches or canes and may stand-up ski with the support of ski boots and outriggers.

L2-3 – Loss of sensation below the level of injury, paralysis/paresis of hip flexors and extensors, knee flexors and extensors, and ankle flexors and extensors. Deficits may involve weakness of inner thigh muscles. Skiers require rigid boots, knee braces, and outriggers. Many are mono-skiers.

T7-T12 – Higher level of sensory loss. Paralysis/paresis includes all of the above, plus loss of muscles of the lower back and stomach, and decreased trunk balance. Most often the person uses a wheelchair for independent mobility and skis using a sit-ski or mono-ski, having fair to good trunk balance and good arm strength, using outriggers for turning and control.

T1-T6 – Paralysis/paresis of all the above plus the loss of upper chest muscles resulting in more loss of trunk balance. The person uses a wheelchair and skis using a sit-ski or bi-ski, or for strong athletes, a mono-ski, with outriggers, often with additional straps to support the upper torso. Quick, smooth turns become more difficult due to less trunk balance.

C8-T1 – Considered quadriplegia/quadriparesis depending on the completeness of injury. This level involves decreased hand function with less ability to flex the fingers and squeeze the hand into a fist, making it difficult to grip ski poles. Other adaptations, such as strapping the outrigger to the hand are often required.

C6-C7 – Includes all the above losses plus weakness of the finger extensors, wrist flexors/extensors, elbow extensors (triceps), and partial weakness of the elbow flexors (biceps). The arm weakness makes it difficult to propel a wheelchair or use any type of ski pole effectively. The skier generally relies more on a tether and ski buddy to help turn the sit-ski or bi-ski.

C5-C6 – Shoulder weakness (deltoids) in addition to all the above losses. Generally the person uses a powered wheelchair. Skiing involves being tethered down the hill in a sit-ski or bi-ski.

C4-C5 and above – Includes all the losses above. People with this level of injury have little physical function except for some head and neck motion. The skier is totally dependent upon a tether for maneuvering down the slope.

Appendix D
Chronicle of the U.S. Disabled Ski Team

1950-1960's: Limited disabled skiing and programs exist in the United States.

Late 1960's: Starting in 1968, most major military hospitals conduct disabled ski programs as part of rehabilitation for servicemen wounded in Vietnam. A joint program between Denver's Children's Hospital and Fitzsimmons Army Hospital helped to spark this development. These programs were modeled after those used in Germany and Austria after World War II.

1972: The first National Disabled Alpine Championships are held in Winter Park, Colorado.

1974: The U.S. Disabled Ski Team, then called the U.S. Handicapped Ski Team, is organized and competed in the first international competition, the World Disabled Alpine Championships, in France.

1974-1980: Minimal participation by the U.S. Team internationally due to lack of organization at the domestic and international levels.

1980: USDST competes in its first Winter Paralympic Games in Geilo, Norway.

1982: USDST competes in the World Disabled Alpine and Nordic Championships. The Alpine Team begins to be competitive with the traditional ski powers: Austria, Germany, and Switzerland.

1984: The USDST competes in the 1984 Winter Paralympic Games held in Innsbruck, Austria. USDST ties with Austria, Germany, and Switzerland for alpine medals won. 1984 becomes a very significant year for disabled skiing, as it is included as an exhibition sport at the 1984 Winter Olympics in Sarajevo, Yugoslavia (now Bosnia), where all three U.S. racers entered won medals.

1986: The USDST competes in the 1986 World Disabled Alpine Championships in Salen, Sweden and wins 59 medals— almost twice as many as second place Germany. The disabled ski team is officially licensed and logoed as the USDST and becomes part of the United States Ski Association (USSA) structure. This action by USSA becomes the model both domestically and internationally for integration of elite disabled sports into the "able-bodied" federation.

1988: At the Winter Paralympic Games in Innsbruck Austria, the USDST retains its number one world ranking. Disabled Skiing is again an exhibition sport in the 1988 Winter Olympic Games held in Calgary, Canada. Of six alpine medals to be won, the USDST wins four, including a sweep in Women's GS and a silver in the Men's GS.

1990: The Alpine World Disabled Championships are held in Winter Park, Colorado. The USDST wins 89 medals, nearly three times as many as second place Germany (37).

1992: The USDST alpine team again took top honors at the Winter Paralympic Games, held in Tignes, France, winning 42 medals including 19 gold. German places second with 22 medals (9 gold).

1994: At the Lillehammer, Norway Paralympic Games, the USDST alpine team retains its number one spot by winning 39 medals (24 gold). Germany again placed second with 32 medals (11 gold).

1996: The World Disabled Alpine Championships are held in Lech, Austria. The United States and Austria tie for total Alpine medals (29), but the USDST won more gold (11).

1998:

At the Nagano Winter Paralympic Games, the USDST Alpine Team again captures top honors by winning 32 medals, including 14 gold. Second place Austria wins 33 (7 gold) and third place Germany wins 15 medals (5 gold).

1998-1999:

The International Ski Federation (FIS) accepts the Disabled Alpine World Cup circuit and establishes a sub-committee for Disabled Alpine competition under the FIS Alpine Committee. At the 1998-99 World Cup Finals in Breckenridge, Colorado, the USDST alpine team is again on top with 25 medals (11 gold), Germany is second with 14 medals (3 gold), and Austria third with 7 medals (2 gold). The U.S. Team also wins the first ever FIS "Nation's Cup" for disabled.

2000:

The World Disabled Ski Championships are hosted by Sion, Switzerland. Alpine events are held in Anzere. The USDST alpine team ranks second with 23 medals (9 gold). Austria places first with 25 medals (4 gold) and Germany places third with 17 medals (10 gold).

1999-2000:

The Disabled Alpine World Cup Circuit begins in Breckenridge, Colorado and ends in Wildschonau, Austria. The World Cup Finals come just a few days after the World Championships. The USDST again claims the FIS Nation's Cup trophy and also wins three of six overall titles. The USDST also won the medal race at the Finals by claiming 18 medals (9 gold). Austria places second with 11 medals (3 gold) and Canada placed third with 7 medals (4 gold).

Appendix E
2001-2002 U.S. Disabled Ski Team Roster

Men's A Team

Clay Fox
Height: 5'7"
Weight: 150 lbs
Birth date: Dec. 24, 1978
Hometown: Gillette, WY
School: Wyoming
Ski club: Winter Park
Disability/Class: B/K amputee/LW4
Disability onset: Age 15 car crash
Started skiing/racing: Age 9/age 16
Year on team: 4th
Career highlights: '00 World Championships GS gold
'00 World Championships SL bronze
Hobbies: Rock climbing
Sponsor: Challenged Athletes, Kennecott Energy

Jason Lalla
Height: 5'11"Weight: 168 lbs
Birth date: May 12, 1971
Hometown: Bradford, NH
School: Northern Colorado
Ski Club: Colorado Disabled Competition Center
Year on team: 5th
Disability/Class: A/K amputee /LW2
Disability onset: Age 18 motorcycle crash
Started skiing/racing: Age 3/age 23
Career highlights: '01 World Cup SL win
'00 World Championships GS gold
'98 Paralympics GS gold
Hobbies: Rock climbing, mountain biking, and hiking
Sponsor: RGP Prosthetics, Vail Valley Foundation, Challenged Athletes
Foundation, Endolite

Chris Waddell
Height: 6'0"
Weight: 150 lbs
Birth date: Sept. 28, 1968
Hometown: Park City, UT
School: Middlebury '91
Ski Club: Berkshire East/National Ability Center
Year on team: 11th
Disability/Class: SCI/LW10
Disability onset: Age 20 skiing mishap
Started skiing/racing: Age 3/age 6
Career highlights: 15 Paralympics and Worlds medals
Five Paralympic gold medals
Three World Championships gold medals
Four Worlds '00 medals (1 gold)
Hobbies: Wheelchair racing
Sponsors: The Hartford, Time-Warner, Yetti, Victorinox/Swiss Army

Men's B Team

Chris Devlin-Young
Height: 5'9"
Weight: 135 lbs
Birth date: December 26, 1961
Hometown: Campton, NH
School: Flathead Valley Community College
Ski Club: New England Disabled Ski Team
Year on team: 8th
Disability/Class: SCI/LW12/1
Disability onset: Age 19/plane crash
Started skiing/racing: Age 10/age 11
Career highlights: '94 Paralympics SL champ
Three World Championships medals
Sponsors: N.E. Disabled Ski Team, White Mountain Adaptive Ski School,
Loon Mountain, Parrot Resorts East/West, Best Buys stores

Monte Meier
Height: 5'10"

Weight: 183 lbs
Birth date: April 27, 1971
Hometown: Hastings, MN
School: Northeast Metro Technical College, '96, Metro State '99
Year on Team: 10th
Disability/Class: A/K amputee/LW2
Disability onset: Age 8 garden tilling accident
Started skiing/racing: Age 9/age 12
Career highlights: Two medals at '00 Worlds
'98 Paralympics SL gold, GS silver
Hobbies: Golf, fishing, hunting, hiking, and camping

Andy Parr
Height: 5'8"
Weight: 170 lbs
Birth date: July 4, 1972
Hometown: Rockland, ME
School: Rockland High School
Ski Club: White Mountain Adaptive Sports of Loon Mountain
Disability/Class: Vision Impairment/B-3
Disability: Age 18 Stargardt's disease
Started skiing/racing: Age 7/age 28
Years on team: 2nd
Guide: David Marchi
Career highlights: Three '01 World Cup podiums
'00 U.S. champ in DH/GS
Hobbies: Mountain biking and hiking

Jacob Rife
Nickname: Jake
Height: 6'0"
Weight: 147 lbs
Birth date: Aug. 1, 1977
Hometown: Pocatello, ID
School: Pocatello High School
Ski Club: Kelly Canyon Ski Team/Sun Valley Disabled
Year on team: 7th
Disability/Class: SCI/LW3

Disability onset: Age 10 hit by a truck while walking
Started skiing/racing: Age 10/age 11
Career highlights: '00 Worlds SL silver
'98 Paralympics SG silver, SL bronze
'96 Worlds DH/SL bronze
Hobbies: Bass and trout fishing
Sponsor: VISA

Men's C Team

Kevin Bramble
Height: 6'2"
Weight: 160 lbs
Birth date: September 19, 1972
Hometown: Truckee, CA
Year on Team: 1st
Disability/Class: SCI/LW12
Disability: Age 21 snowboarding accident
Started skiing/racing: Age 11/age 25
Career highlights: 2nd in an unofficial World Cup at Breckenridge
'98 U.S. super G champ
Hobbies: Design and build all sports equipment, kayaking, mountain biking
1998 World Cup Finals 2nd DH
World Cup Snowbasin 1st DH

Adam Fromma
Height: 5'7"
Weight: 175 lbs
Birth date: Oct. 15, 1974
Hometown: Winter Park, CO
Ski Club: Club: Jiminy Peak/Winter Park
Disability/Class: U/E amputee/LW6
Disability Onset: Congenital
Years on Team: 5th
Started skiing/racing: Age 12/age 21
Career highlights: '01 U.S. Nationals 4th in DH, and SG, bronze GS
Ninth in downhill at '00 Worlds

Sixth in unofficial World Cup slalom at Breckenridge in '99 season
14th in first official World Cup at Breckenridge,
Ninth in '98 Paralympic slalom, 10th in GS and 12th in DH
Hobbies: Hiking, camping, mountain biking, and golf

Dan Kosick
Nickname: Danimal
Height: 6'0"
Weight: 180 lbs
Birth date: Aug. 16, 1977
Hometown: Binghamton, NY
School: Binghamton University '00
Ski Club: Club: Greek Peak/Winter Park
Year on Team: 5th
Disability/Class: A/K amputee LW2
Disability: Age 15 cancer
Started skiing/racing: Age 9/age 16
Career highlights: Fourth in a WC slalom at Breckenridge in '00
Fourth in the 1998 Paralympic DH in Nagano
Seventh in DH at Obersaxon, Switzerland World Cup 2001
Four other World Cup top 10 finishes
Hobbies: Scuba diving, road and mountain biking

Joe Tompkins
Height: 6'5"
Weight: 226 lbs
Birth date: Aug. 20, 1968
Hometown: Juneau, AK
Ski Club: NSCD/Winter Park
Disability/Class: SCI/LW10
Disability: Age 20 automobile accident
Started skiing/racing: Age 14/age 25
Years on team: 3rd
Career highlights: Won the inaugural official World Cup race, a DH, at Breckenridge '99
Sixth in DH at '00 Worlds
Third in super G, fifth in GS at Breckenridge's '99 unofficial World Cup
Second in SG, fourth in SL at '99 Chevy Astro U.S. Championships

Hobbies: Golf, fishing, and kayaking
Sponsors: Juneau Sport Fishing, Juneau Lions Club, SeAlaska

Women's A Team

Sarah Billmeier
Height: 5'10"
Weight: 130 lbs
Birth date: June 13, 1977
Birthplace: Brattleboro, VT
Hometown: Yarmouth, ME
School: Dartmouth '01
Year on Team: 11th
Disability/Class: A/K amputee/LW2
Disability: Age 5 cancer
Started skiing/racing: Age 8/age 10
Career highlights: Three World Championships golds
Six-time world champion
Seven-time Paralympics champion
Hobbies: Painting still-lifes, kayaking, canoeing, soccer, and lacrosse

Muffy Davis
Height: 5'10"
Weight: 135 lbs
Birth date: Dec. 1, 1972
Birthplace: Ann Arbor, MI
Hometown: Sun Valley, ID
School: Stanford '95
Ski Club: Sun Valley Ski Team/Park City Ski Team
Year on team: 5th
Disability/Class: SCI/LW10
Disability onset: Age 16 ski accident
Started skiing/racing: Age 3/age 7
Career highlights: Three World Cup titles in '01
'00 World Championships GS gold
'98 Paralympic bronze medal, slalom
Hobbies: River rafting, scuba diving, horseback riding, handcycling,
camping, and watching movies.

Lee Joiner
Height: 5'8"
Weight: 125 lbs
Birth date: Oct. 19, 1981
Hometown: Red Lodge, MT
School: Red Lodge High School
Year on Team: 4th
Started skiing/racing: Age 7/age 12
Disability/Class: A/K amputee, shortened arm/LW9
Disability onset: Congenital shortened arm, A/K amputee
Career highlights: U.S. slalom champion
Two top-5s at '00 Worlds
Hobbies: Golf

Csilla Kristof
Nickname: Chee
Height: 5'5"
Weight: 135 lbs
Birth date: Aug. 3, 1984
Hometown: Las Vegas, NV
School: Burke Mt. Academy
Ski Club: Burke Mt. Academy
Year on team: 4th
Disability/Class: U/E amputee/LW6
Disability onset: Congenital
Started skiing/racing: Age 3/age 9
Career highlights: Four World Cup thirds in '01
'00 World Championships DH bronze
Won first official World Cup '01
Hobbies: Soccer, running, music, and tanning
Sponsor: Pratte Development

Allison Pearl
Height: 5'6"
Weight: 135 lbs
Birth date: June 13, 1975
Hometown: Reno, Nevada

School: University of Nevada '97, '01
Ski Club: Winter Park Disabled Ski Team
Year on team: 1st
Disability/Class: Paraplegia/LW12-1
Disability onset: Blood clot age 18
Starting skiing/racing: Age 5/age 5
Career highlights: Three '01 World Cup wins
U.S super G champ
Hobbies: Hand cycling, swimming, and hiking

Mary Riddell
Height: 5'2"
Weight: 128 lbs
Birth date: Feb. 15, 1980
Hometown: Dove Creek, CO
School: Vail Valley Academy
Ski Club: Purgatory Race Team, Durango/Purgatory Adaptive Sports
Assn.
Year on Team: 8th
Disability/Class: B/K amputee/LW4
Disability onset7: Congenital
Started skiing/racing: Age 4/age 9
Career highlights: '00, '01 World Cup overall champ
'00 Worlds: three medals (one gold)
'98 Paralympics: four medals (one gold)
'96 Worlds: three medals (two gold)

Sarah Will
Height: 5'1"
Weight: 99 lbs
Birth date: June 10, 1965
Birthplace: Suffern, NY
Hometown: Vail, CO
Year on Team: 11th
School: Green Mountain '86
Ski Club: Ski Club Vail
Disability/Class: SCI/LW11
Disability onset: Age 24 skiing mishap

Started skiing/racing: Age 4/age 9
Career highlights: '01 World Cup SG champ
'00 World Cup overall/SL/GS champ
Gold/silver/bronze at '00 Worlds
Eight Paralympics, three Worlds gold medals
Hobbies: Painting, downhill wheelchair racing

Women's B Team

Allison Marie Jones
Nickname: Jonezy
Height: 5'5"
Weight: 130 lbs
Birth date: May 12, 1984
Birthplace: Amarillo, TX
Hometown: Colorado Springs, CO
School: Middle Park High School
Ski Club: Winter Park Disabled Ski Team
Disabled Class: LW2
Disability onset: Congenital
Started skiing/racing: Age 5/age 8
Year on team: 2nd
Hobbies: Cycling
Career Highlights: Five World Cup top-10's
Hobbies: Cycling and listening to music

Women's C Team

Sandy Dukat
Height: 5'7"
Weight: 130
Birth date: May 3, 1972
Hometown: Canton, OH
School: Wittenberg University '94
Ski Club: NSCD, Winter Park, CO
Year on team: 1st
Disability/Class: A/K amputee/ LW2
Disability onset: Congenital

Started skiing/racing: Age 25/ age 25
Career highlights: 7th at '01 World Cup DH and GS in Kimberly Canada
Hobbies: Running, cycling, kayaking, and all outdoor activities
Sponsor: The Rehabilitation Institute of Chicago

Lacey Heward
Height: 5'8"
Weight: 110 lbs
Birth date: Nov. 27, 1979
Hometown: Boise, Idaho
School: Capital High School
Ski Club: Park City
Disability/Class: SCI/LW11
Disability onset: 16 months barbell accident
Started skiing/racing: Age 15/age 19
Year on Team: 1st
Career Highlights: 1st at '01 World Cup slalom in Kimberly Canada
Hobbies: Music

Jennifer Kelchner
Height: 5'4"
Weight: 128 lbs
Birth date: Jan. 29, 1979
Hometown: Cazenovia, NY
Disability/Class: B/K Amputee/LW4
Disability: Age 4 lawn mower mishap
Year on Team: 5th
Started skiing/racing: Age 2
Career Highlights: '98 Paralympics DH gold
'98 Nationals super G and GS champ
Overall champ at '98 Nationals
'98 Canadian super G gold medalist
Overall champion at '98 Canadian Nationals

Appendix F
Disability Classification System

LW1 – Athletes with two disabled legs who ski with two skis and two stabilizers*.
- two above-the-knee prostheses, skiing with two normal skis and two stabilizers
- one below-knee prosthesis and an above-the-knee amputation skiing with one normal ski and two stabilizers
- disability in both lower limbs other than amputation skiing with two normal or different skis and two stabilizers

LW2 – Athletes with one disabled leg who ski with one ski and two stabilizers.
- a single above-the-knee or below-the-knee amputation, or at least 30 point muscular weakness in one limb or equivalent disability skiing with two stabilizers plus one normal ski
- disability in one leg skiing with two stabilizers, one normal ski, and one attached small ski
- a support for one disabled leg, one normal ski and two stabilizers

LW3 – Athletes with two disabled legs who ski with two skis and two stabilizers.
- disabilities in both legs, less severe than LW1, skiing with two normal skis and two stabilizers
- double below-the-knee amputees skiing with two normal skis and two stabilizers
- disabilities in both legs with muscular weakness between 15 to 44 points or equivalent disability skiing with two normal skis and two stabilizers

LW4 – Athletes with one disabled leg who ski with two skis and two stabilizers (lesser disability than for category LW2).
- a single below or above-the-knee amputation with prosthesis
- muscular weakness or paralysis with a decrease of strength of at least 10 points or equivalent disability

- totally blocked knee
- totally blocked hip
- bilateral foot amputations or disability

LW 5/7 – Athletes using two normal skis, but with two disabled arms, making it impossible to use stabilizers.
- disabilities in both arms skiing with two normal skis and no stabilizers
- amputation of both arms
- weakness, paralysis or deformity of both arms
(Athletes are allowed to use prostheses or orthoses if they desire.)
- LW 6/8 – Athletes with one disabled arm, making it impossible to use more than one pole, skiing with two normal skis.
- disability in one arm, skiing with two normal skis and one stabilizer
- one-arm amputation
- weakness, paralysis, or deformity of one arm
(Athletes are allowed to use prostheses or orthosis.)

LW9 – Athletes with disabilities to an arm or leg, skiing with equipment of their choice using two skis.
- Those disabled in one arm and one leg on the same side.
- Those disabled in one arm and one opposite leg.

LW10 – Athletes with two disabled legs and no functional sitting balance using a mono-ski and athletes with impaired legs along with a functional trunk impairment.

LW11 – Athletes with two disabled legs with sitting balance using a mono-ski and athletes with the ability to stand but with impairment of both legs along with functional impairment of the trunk and/or hips.

LW12 – Athletes with two disabled legs and good sitting balance using a mono-ski. Visually impaired

B1 – Partially blind. Ski with two skis and two poles. Can distinguish between light and dark, but not shapes.

B2 – Partially sighted. Ski with two skis and two poles. Best correctable vision up to 20/600 and/or visual field of five degrees.

B3 – Partially sighted. Ski with two skis and two poles. Best corrected vision from 20/600 to 20/200 and/or field of vision from five to 20 degrees.

*Stabilizers may be either poles or outriggers.

Appendix G
Adaptive Ski Programs

The following ski areas and organizations offer adaptive skiing programs. These range from programs with full services seven days a week throughout the ski season including adaptive equipment rental, PSIA (Professional Ski Instructors of America) certified instructors, lessons, and racing opportunities to instruction-only facilities for those who can provide their own equipment limited to one or two days a week. Costs vary, with many areas providing reduced-price lift tickets and/or lessons for the disabled. Always call in advance to find out what is available and to make reservations. Many other areas teach people with disabilities on a one-to-one basis and others plan to add adaptive ski programs in the future.

ALASKA

Alpine Alternatives
2518 E. Tudor Rd., Suite 105
Anchorage, AK 99507
Phone: 907-561-6655
Phone: 800-361-4174
Email: info@alpinealternatives.org
Web Site: www.alpinealternatives.org

Alyeska Resort (See Challenge Alaska)
PO Box 249
Girdwood, AK 99587
Phone: 907-754-1111
Web Site: www.alyeskaresort.com

Challenge Alaska
PO Box 11065
Anchorage, Alaska 99511
Phone: 888-430-2738
Phone: 907-344-7399
Adaptive ski school: 907-783-2925
Email: challenge.alaska@acsalaska.net

Web Site: www.challenge.ak.org

Eaglecrest Ski Area (See ORCA)
155 S. Seward St.
Juneau, AK 99801
Phone: 907 586-5284
Email: ecrestak@alaska.net
Web Site: www.juneau.lib.ak.us/community/orca/index.htm

Outdoor Recreation and Community Access (ORCA)
PO Box 35134
Juneau, AK 99803
Phone: 907-586-0104
Email: sailinc@ptialaska.net
Web Site: www.juneau.lib.ak.us/community/orca/index.htm

ARIZONA

Mesa Association of Sports for the Disabled
PO Box 4727
Mesa, AZ 85211-4727
Phone: 480-472-0638
Email: gjbaumga@mpsaz.org

CALIFORNIA

Alpine Meadows
PO Box 5279
Tahoe City, CA 95730
Phone: 530-583-4232
Email: dsusatahoe@truckee.net
Web Site: www.skialpine.com

Badger Pass Ski Area
Glacier Point Road
Yosemite, CA 95389
Phone: 209-372-8430 ext.1189
Email: stewartcollins@dncinc.com

Web Site: www.BadgerPass.com

Bear Valley Mountain Resort
PO Box 5038
Bear Valley CA 95223
Phone: 209-753-2301
Web Site: www.caohwy.com/b/bearvski.htm

Big Bear Mountain Ski & Summer Resort
PO Box 6812
43101 Goldmine Drive
Big Bear Lake, CA 92315
Phone: 909-585-2519
Email: bearmtn@boothcreek.com
Web Site: www.bearmtn.com
See United States Adaptive Recreation Center

Discovery Blind Sports
27685 North Chaparral Court
Pioneer, CA 95666
Phone: 209-295-3641
Email: natcraig@volcano.net
Web Site: www.discoverysports.org
Offers skiing at Kirkwood Mountain Resort

Kirkwood Mountain Resort
1501 Kirkwood Meadows Drive
Kirkwood, CA 95646.
Phone: 209-258-6000
Email: kwd-info@skikirkwood.com
Web Site: www.kirkwood.com
See Discovery Blind Sports

Mammoth Adaptive Sports School
PO Box 7615
Mammoth Lakes, CA 93546
Phone: 760-934-2571 ext. 3258
Email: ktaketomo@mammoth-mtn.com

Web Site: www.familytravelguides.com/articles/skiing/mammoth.html

Snow Summit Mountain Resort
880 Summit Blvd.
PO Box 77
Big Bear Lake, CA 92315
Phone: 909-866-5766
Email: info@snowsummit.com
Web Site: www.snowsummit.com/

Tahoe Adaptive Ski School
Disabled Sports USA, Far West
PO Box 9780
Truckee, CA 96162
Phone: 530-581-4161
Email: dsusatah@truckee.net
Web Site: www.dsusafw.org

U.S. Adaptive Recreation Center
PO Box 2897
Big Bear Lake, CA 92315
Phone: 909-584-0269
Email: mail@usarc.org
Web Site: www.usarc.org
Offers skiing at Big Bear

COLORADO

Adaptive Sports Association of Durango
PO Box 1884
Durango, CO 81302
Reservation Phone: 970-385-2163
Administrative Office Phone: 970-259-0374
Email: asa@frontier.net
Web Site: www.asadurango.org/winter.html

Adaptive Sports Center of Crested Butte
PO Box 1639

Crested Butte, CO 81224
Phone: 970-349-2296
Phone: 866-349-2296
Email: info@adaptivesports.org
Web Site: www.adaptivesports.org

Beaver Creek Resort
Beaver Creek, Colorado
PO Box 7
Vail, CO 81658
Phone: 800-427-8308
Email: bcinfo@vailresorts.com
Web Site: www.beavercreek.com

Blind Outdoor Leisure Development (BOLD)
533 E. Main
Aspen, CO 81661
Phone: 970-925-9511

Breckenridge Outdoor Education Center
Breckenridge Ski Area
Breckenridge, CO 80424
Phone: 970-453-5633
Email: skiprog@BOEC.org
Web Site: BOEC.org

Challenge Aspen
PO Box M
Aspen, CO 81612
Phone: 970-923-0578
Email: possibilities@challengeaspen.com
Web Site: www.aspensnowmass.com

Colorado Blind Skiing
Box 558
Avon, CO 81620
Phone: 303-949-4848

Colorado Discover Ability and Integrated Outdoor Adventures
366 Plateau Drive
Grand Junction, CO 81503
Phone: 970-268-5700 ext. 2037
Phone: 970-245-4992, Tyler Jones, Program Director
Email: ski@powderhorn.com
Web Site: www.powderhorn.com
Offers skiing at Powderhorn Ski Area

Crested Butte Adaptive Ski Program
PO Box 1639
Crested Butte, CO 81224
Phone: 970-349-2296
Email: ascl@csn.net

Cuchara Mountain Sports Center for the Disabled
25069 County Road BB
La Junta, CO 81050
Phone: 719-384-6580
Email: RoycethePT@juno.com

Eldora Special Recreation Program
PO Box 19016
Boulder, CO 80308-2016
Phone: 303-442-0606
Email: eldora@eldora.com
Web Site: www.esrp.org

Keystone Resort/Keystone Mountain
PO Box 38K45
Keystone, CO 80435
Phone: 970-468-2316
Web Site: www.snow.com
Program run through BOEC

National Sports Center for the Disabled
PO Box 1290
Winter Park, CO 80482

Phone: 970-726-1540
Email: dnichols@nscd.org
Web Site: www.nscd.org
Web Site: www.skiwinterpark.com

Steamboat Ski Area
2305 Mount Warner Circle
Steamboat Springs, CO 80487
Phone: 800-922-2722
Phone: 970-879-6111 ext. 3528
Email: info@steamboat-ski.com
Web Site: www.steamboat.com

Telluride Adaptive Ski Program
PO Box 2254
Telluride, CO 81435
Phone: 970-728-7537
Email: tasp@telluridecolorado.net
Web Site: www.skitasp.org

Vail Adaptive Program
Golden Peak Ski School
PO Box 7
Vail, CO 81658
Phone: 970-479-3264
Web Site: vail.snow.com/m.ssschool.adaptive.asp

CONNECTICUT

Connecticut Handicapped Ski Association
Powderidge Ski Resort
Middlefield, CT 06451
Phone: 203-248-2242

GEORGIA

Disabled Sports USA-Atlanta
4903 Judith Avenue

Acworth, GA 30109
Phone: 770-917-1258
Email: k.anderson@mindspring.com

IDAHO

PASS (Pocatello Adaptive Ski School)
Cooperative Wilderness Handicapped Outdoor Group (C.W.HOG).
Box 8128
Pocatello, ID 83209
Phone: 208-282-3912
Email: dayljust@isu.edu
Web Site: www.isu.edu/cwhog
Offers skiing at Pebble Creek Ski Area

Recreation Unlimited, Inc.
1610 North Orchard
Boise, ID 83706
Phone: 208-672-1500
Phone: 208-383-0210 John Summerton
Email: rkrogh@micron.net
Web Site: www.recreation-unlimited.org
Offers adaptive skiing at Bogus Basin Ski area

Sun Valley Adaptive Sports Program, Inc.
PO Box 6791
Ketchum, ID 83340
Business Phone: 208-726-9298
Phone: 208 726-9013, Marc Mast
Email: Svas@sunvalley.net
Web Site: www.svasp.org

ILLINOIS

The American Blind Skiing Foundation
227 E. North Ave.
Elmhurst, IL 60126
Email: ABSF@bigfoot.com

Web Site: www.absf.org
RIC-Skiers
Rehabilitation Institute of Chicago's Center for Health & Fitness
710 North Lakeshore Drive
Chicago, IL 60611
Phone: 312-908-4292
Email: ricsport@megsinet.net

INDIANA

Special Outdoor Leisure Opportunities [SOLO], Inc.
PO Box 6221
South Bend, IN 46660
Phone: 219-291-7814

MAINE

Maine Adaptive Sports and Recreation
174 Maine Street
Bangor, ME 04401
Phone: 888-877-8305
Email: Pelle@agate.net
Web Site: www.maineadaptivesports.com
Offers skiing at New Hermon Mountain

Maine Handicapped Skiing
Sunday River
8 Sundance Lane
Newry, ME 04261
Phone: 207-824-2440
Phone: 800-639-7770
Email: info@skimhs.org
Web Site: www.skimhs.org

Sugarloaf/USA
RR1 Box 5000
Carrabassett Valley, ME 04947
Phone: 207-237-2000

Email: info@sugarloaf.com
Web Site: www.sugarloaf.com/company/contact.html
(see Maine Handicapped Skiing)

MARYLAND

Baltimore Adapted Recreation and Sports [BARS]
PO Box 878
Sparks, MD 21152
Phone: 410-771-4606
Email: Pam4bars@aol.com

Nation's Capital Handicapped Sports
PO Box 1546
Olney, MD 20830-1546
Phone: 301-657-3277
Adaptive skiing at Whitetail, PA

Wisp Ski Area
PO Box 629
McHenry, MD 21541
Phone: 301-387-4911
Email: wispinfo@gcnet.net
Web Site: www.gcnet.net/wisp/ski/ski-rate.htm

MASSACHUSETTS

Child & Family Services
Adaptive Sports & REC (Recreation, Education, and Competition)
367 Pine Street
Springfield, MA 01105
Phone: 413-788-9695
Email: rec135@cfs.org

Jiminy Peak Adaptive Ski program
37 Corey Road
Hancock, MA 01237
Phone: 413-738-5500 (Mountain)

Phone: 518-462-6683 (STRIDE Reservations)
Web Site: pages.prodigy.net/redmax1/ski.htm

Wachusett Mountain
499 Mountain Road
Princeton, MA 01541
Phone: 978-464-2300 ext. 3718
Email: krshea@abilityplus.org
Web Site: www.wachusett.com

MICHIGAN

Cannonsburg Adaptive Ski Association
Cannonsburg Ski Lodge
6800 Cannonsburg Road NE
Belmont, MI 49306
Phone: 616-874-6711

Challenge Mountain of Walloon Hills
PO Box 735
Boyne City, MI 49712
Phone: 616-535-2141
Email: cmski@unnet.com
Web Site: www.challengemtn.org

Michigan Adaptive Sports
PO Box 240368
Orchard Lake, MI 48324-0368
Phone: 248-988-0156
Email: michadaptivesports@kozmail.com
Web Site: www.mihometown.com/oe/mas

MINNESOTA

Buena Vista Ski Area
621 Lake Julia Drive NW
Bemidji, MN 56601
Phone: 218-243-2231

Phone: 763-520-0495, Karyl Hoeger, Courage Center
Web Site: www.skiagent.com/overview.cfm/mn04.htm

Courage Center
424 West Superior Street, #200
Duluth, MN 55802
Phone: 218-726-4763
Email: couraged@computerpro.com
Offers program at Spirit Mountain

Courage Center
3915 Golden Valley Road
Minneapolis, MN 55422
Phone: 763-520-0520
Phone: 888-8INTAKE
Web Site: www.courage.org

Hyland Ski & Snowboard Area
8800 Chalet Road
Bloomington, MN 55438-1209
Phone: 952-835-4250
Phone 952-835-4604, Jean White, Courage Center
Web Site: www.hylandski.com
(See Courage Center, Minneapolis)

Spirit Mountain Recreation Area
9500 Spirit Mountain Place
Duluth, MN 55810
Phone: 218-628-2891
Phone: 218-726-4762, Eric Larson, Courage Center
(See Courage Center, Duluth)

Welch Village Ski Area
PO Box 146
Welch, MN 55089
Phone: 651-222-7079
Phone: 651-222-7079, Bev Hawkinson, Courage Center
Email: welchVillage@usinternet.com

Web Site: www.welchvillage.com
(See Courage Center, Minneapolis)

MONTANA

Big Sky Resort
PO Box 16000 1
1 Lone Mountain Trail
Big Sky, MT 59716
Web Site: www.bigskyresort.com

Dream Disabled Ski Program
PO Box 7774
Kalispell, MT 59904
Phone: 406-752-8903
Email: oneil@in-tch.com
Offers skiing at Big Mountain Resort
PO Box 1400
Whitefish, MT 59937
Phone: 406-862-1817
Email: bigmtn@bigmtn.com
Web Site: www.bigmtn.com/html/disabled.html

Eagle Mount Billings
2822 3rd Avenue North, Suite 203
Billings, MT 59101
Phone: 406-245-5422

Eagle Mount Bozeman
6901 Goldenstein Lane
Bozeman, MT 59715
Phone: 800-858-8968

Eagle Mount Great Falls
#9 3rd Street North, Suite 1
Great Falls, MT 59401
Phone: 406-454-1449
Email: eaglemount@mcn.net

Web Site: www.mcn.net/eaglemount

Eagle Mount – Missoula
Phone: 406-543-7321

NEVADA

Heavenly Ski Resort
P.O. Box 2180
Stateline, NV 89449
Phone: 775-586-7000
Email: info@skiheavenly.com
Web Site: www.skiheavenly.com

Sky Tavern Jr. Ski Program
P.O. Box 1709
Reno, Nevada 89505-1709
Phone: 702-323-5125

NEW HAMPSHIRE

AbilityPLUS at Attitash/Bear Peak
P.O. Box 308 Route #302
Bartlett, NH 03850
Phone: 603-374-2688, Beth Davis, Program Director
Phone: 603-374-2368, mountain
Email: bdavis250@hotmail.com
Web Site: www.abilityplus.org/skiprogs.html

AbilityPLUS Inc.
P.O. Box 253
Waterville Valley, NH 03215
Phone: 978-365-6200
Phone: 978-365-6230
Email: Info@abilityplus.org
Web Site: www.abilityplus.org

Bretton Woods Adaptive Ski Program

Route 302
Bretton Woods, NH 03575
Phone: 603-278-3000
Phone: 603-278-3398, Adaptive Program
Email: adaptiveprogram@brettonwoods.com
Web Site: www.abilityplus.org/skiprogs.html

Gunstock
Rte. 11A
Gilford, NH 03249
Phone: 800-GUNSTOCK
Email: gunstock@gunstock.com
Web Site: www.gunstock.com

King Pine Ski Area
Route 153 HC 63
Box 40
East Madison, NH 03849
Phone: 603-367-8896
Email: info@purityspring.com
Web Site: www.kingpine.com

Mount Sunapee Resort
P.O. Box 2021
Newbury, NH 03255
Phone: 603-763-2356
Email: info@mtsunapee.com
Web Site: www.mtsunapee.com

New England Handicapped Sports Association (NEHSA)
PO Box 2135
Newbury, NH 03255-2135
Or
P.O. Box 2135
Mt. Sunapee, NH 03255
Phone: 603-763-9158
Phone: 800-628-4484
Email: nehsa@sugar-river.net

Web Site: www.nehsa.org

Northeast Passage
Hewitt Hall
4 Library Way
Durham, NH 03824
Phone: 603-862-0070
Email: northeast.passage@unh.edu
Web Site: www.nepassage.org/home.htm
Offers skiing at areas all over the Northeast and equipment rental

The Waterville Valley Adaptive Skiing Program
P.O. Box 253
Town Square
Waterville Valley, NH 03215
Phone: 603-236-8311 ext. 3175
Email: Info@abilityplus.org
Web Site: www.waterville.com/winter/adaptive.html

The White Mountain Adaptive Ski School
Loon Mountain Resort
RR1 Box 41
Kancamagus Hwy.
Lincoln, NH 03251-9711
Phone: 603-745-6281 ext. 5663
Email: wmass@bdol.com
Web Site: www.loonmtn.com/winter/adaptive.html

NEW MEXICO

Angel Fire Resort
P.O. Drawer B
Angel Fire, NM 87710
Phone: 505-377-4207
Email: sb@angelfireresort.com
Web Site: www.angelfireresort.com

Challenge New Mexico

2504 Camino Entrada
Santa Fe, NM 87505
Phone: 505-988-7621
Email: cnm@challengenewmexico.com
Web Site: www.uwsfc.org/pages/cnm.html

New Mexico Adaptive Ski Program
1304 Calle Joya
Santa Fe, NM 87501
Phone: 505-995-9858
Email: Christi.Hield@Juno.com
Web Site: adaptiveski.org
Offers skiing at Sandia Peak and Santa Fe Ski areas

Sante Fe Ski Area
Santa Fe, NM 87501
Phone: 505-982-4429
Web Site: www.skisantefe.com
See New Mexico Adaptive Ski Program

Ski Apache Handicapped Association
Ski Apache
P.O. Box 220
Ruidoso, NM 88355
Phone: 505-336-4356
Email: sschool@skiapache.com
Web Site: www.skiapache.com

NEW YORK

Adaptive Ski Program at Ski Windham NY
P.O. Box 459
Windham, NY 12496
Phone: 518-734-4300
Email: asfwindham@aol.com
Web Site: www.skiwindham.com

The Bill Lounsbury Adaptive Ski Program

Holiday Valley Resort
P.O. Box 370
Ellicottville, New York 14731
Phone: 716-699-2345 ext. 4413
Email: skiing@holidayvalley.com
Web Site: www3.sympatico.ca/fitter/ski.html

Bristol Mountain
5662 Route 64
Canadaigua, NY 14424
Phone: 716-374-6000
Email: Info@Bristolmt.com
Web Site: www.bristolmountain.com

Gore Mountain Ski Area
P.O. Box 470
North Creek, NY 12853
Phone: 518-251-2411
Email: mail@goremountain.com
Web Site: www.goremountain.com

Greek Peak Adaptive Ski Program
2000 NYS Rte. 392
Cortland, NY 13045
Phone: 800-955-2SKI
Phone: 607-657-8317, Peggy Anderson
Email: greekpeak@lightlink.com
Web Site: www.greekpeak.net

The Double "H" Hole in the Woods Ranch
97 Hidden Valley Road
Lake Luzerne, NY 12846
Phone: 518-696-5676, Wendy Clarke, Ski Program Coordinator
Email: theranch@doublehranch.org.
Web Site: www.doublehranch.org/ski_program.html

Hunter Mountain Ski Bowl
P.O. Box 295

Hunter, NY 12442
Phone: 518-263-4223
Email: postmaster@huntermtn.com
Web Site: www.huntermtn.com

Kissing Bridge
P.O. Box 73
Glenwood, NY 14069
Phone: 716-592-4963
Phone: 716-648-6895, Nancy Maressa
Email: debbieg@kbemail.com
Web Site: www.kissing-bridge.com

S.T.R.I.D.E
P.O. Box 778
Rensselaer, NY 12144
Phone: 518-283-2114
Email: redmax1@prodigy.net
Web Site: pages.prodigy.net/redmax1

Whiteface Mt. Adaptive Ski Program
P.O. Box 198
Wilmington, NY 12997
Phone: 518-946-2223
Email ordaws@northnet.org
Web Site: www.orda.org

OHIO

The Adaptive Adventure Sports Coalition
833 Eastwind Drive
Westerville, OH 43081
Phone: 614-823-7156

Boston Mills/Brandywine Ski Resort
P.O. Box 175
Peninsula, OH 44264-0175
Phone: 800-875-4241

Email: info@bmbw.com
Web Site: www.bmbw.com

Madriver Mountain
TAASC
P.O. Box 22
Bellefontaine, OH 43311
Phone: 937-599-1015
Email: sales@skimadness.com

Three Trackers of Ohio
P O Box 44121
Cleveland, OH 44144
Phone: 216-556-0787
Email: MD1053@aol.com

Youth Challenge
Sports and Recreation for Children With Physical Disabilities
4320 West 220 Street
Cleveland, OH 44126
Phone: 440-331-2050
Email: youthchallenge@drfast.net
Web Site: www.youthchallengesports.com

OREGON

Alpine Adventures
Hilyard Community Center
2580 Hilyard
Eugene, OR 97405
Phone: 541-682-6304
Email: kellie.l.kehrein@ci.eugene.or.us
Web Site: www.ci.eugene.or.us

Challenge Oregon adaptive Ski Program
P.O. Box 943
Bend, Oregon 97702
Phone: 541-383-4278

Email: coasp@adaptive-skiing.org
Web Site: www.adaptive-skiing.org

Mt. Bachelor Ski Resort
335 SW Century Drive
Bend, Oregon 97702
Phone: 541-382-2442
Phone: 800.829.2442
Email info@mtbachelor.com
Web Site: www.mtbachelor.com

Timberline Ski School
Timberline Lodge
Timberline, OR 97028
Phone: 503-231-5400 x414
Contact: Ski School
Email: skischool@timberlinelodge.com
Web Site: www.timberlinelodge.com

Willamette Pass
P.O. Box 5509
Eugene, OR 97405
Phone: 541-345-7669
Email: snowinfo@willamettepass.com
Web Site: willamettepass.com
Adaptive skiing through Alpine Adventures

PENNSYLVANIA

Camelback Ski Area
P.O. Box 168
Tannersville, PA 18372
Phone: 570-629-1661
Email: sales@skicamelback.com
Web Site: www.skicamelback.com

Jack Frost/Big Boulder
P.O. Box 707

Blakeslee, PA 18610
Phone: 570-443-8425, ext. 2503
Email: tracys@jackfrostbigboulder.com
Web Site: jackfrostbigboulder.com

Liberty Mountain Resort and Conference Center
P O Box SKI
Carroll Valley, PA 17320
Phone: 717-642-8282
Email: skiliberty@skiliberty.com
Web Site: www.skiliberty.com

Pennsylvania Center for Adaptive Sports
4 Boathouse Row
Philadelphia, PA 19130
Phone: 215-765-5118
Email: pacenter@aol.com
Web Site: www.centeronline.com/index.html

Three Rivers Adaptive Sports
P O Box 38235
Pittsburgh, PA 15238
Phone: 412-749-2281
Email: markk@otwatson.org

Western PA, BOLD
Box 2574, Pittsburgh 15230
Phone: 412-882-3965
Email: bold@trfn.clpgh.org
Web Site: trfn.clpgh.org/bold

Whitetail Resort
13805 Blairs Valley Road
Mercersburg, PA 17236
Phone: 717-328-9400
Email: skiwhitetail@skiwhitetail.com
Web Site: www.skiwhitetail.com

RHODE ISLAND

Shake-A-Leg Providence, RI.
P.O. Box 1264
Newport, RI 02840
Phone: 401-849-8898
Email: shake@shakealeg.org
Web Site: www.shakealeg.org

UTAH

The Canyons
4000 The Canyons Resort Drive
Park City, UT 84098
Phone: 435-649-5400
Email: keldridge@thecanyons.com
Web Site: thecanyons.com
Offers instruction in conjunction with the National Ability Center

National Ability Center
P.O. Box 682799
3351 N. Hwy 248
Park City, Utah 84069-2799
Phone: 435-649-3991
Email: nac@xmission.com
Web Site: www.nationalabilitycenter.org
Offers skiing through Park City Mountain Resort

Options for Independence
1095 North Main
Logan, UT 84341
Phone: 435-753-5353

Snowbird Ski and Summer Resort
P.O. Box 929000
Snowbird, UT 84092-9000
Phone: 801-742-2222
Phone: 800-232-9542

Email: info@snowbird.com
Web Site: www.snowbird.com

VERMONT

AbilityPLUS Inc.
Mt. Snow Adaptive Skiing Program
Mount Snow, Vermont
Phone: 802-464-1100 ext. 4699, Will Wohnus, Director
Email: adaptiveclinics@mountsnow.com
Web Site: www.abilityplus.org/skiprogs.html

Ascutney Mountain Resort
P.O. Box 699
Brownsville, VT 05037
Phone: 802-484-7711
Email: info@ascutney.net
Web Site: www.ascutney.com/winter/index.phtml
(See VASS)

Bromley Mountain
P.O. Box 1130
Manchester Center, VT 05255
Phone: 802-824-5522
Email: prostaff@sover.net
Web Site: www.bromley.com

Killington Resort
4763 Killington Road
Killington, VT 05751
Phone: 800-621-MTNS
Email: info@killington.com
Web Site: www.killington.com/html
(See VASS)

Okemo Mountain Resort
77 Okemo Ridge Road
Ludlow, VT 05149

Phone: 802-228-4041
Email: info@okemo.com
Web Site: www.okemo.com

Sugarbush Resort
2405 Sugarbush Access Road
Warren, VT 05674
Phone: 800-53-SUGAR
Email: info@sugarbush.com
Web Site: www.sugarbush.com/html
(see VASS)

VASS (Vermont Adaptive Ski and Sports)
P.O. Box 139
Killington, VT 05751
Phone: 802-786-4991
Email: office@vermontadaptive.org
Web Site: www.vermontadaptive.org
Offers skiing at Killington, Sugarbush Resort, and Ascutney Mountain

VIRGINIA

The Homestead
U.S. Route 220 Main Street
P.O. Box 2000
Hot Springs, VA 24445
Phone: 800-838-1766
Email: Homestead.info@ourclub.com
Web Site: www.thehomestead.com

Massanutten Resort
P.O. Box 1227
Harrisonburg, VA 22801
Phone: 800-207-MASS
Email: skimass@shentelnet
Web Site: www.massresort.com

Wintergreen Adaptive Skiing

P.O. Box 56
Batesville Va. 22924
Phone: 804-325-2007
Email: info@skiwas.org
Web Site: www.skiwas.org

WASHINGTON

Alpental Ski Area
Snoqualmie, WA 98068
Web Site: skigeeks.com/index.html

Crystal Mountain
33914 Crystal Mountain Blvd.
Crystal Mountain, WA 98022
Phone: 360-663-2265
Email: comments@skicrystal.com
Web Site: www.crystalmt.com/static/index.cfm

Disabled Sports USA Northwest - "Team USAble"
20015 SE 95th ST
Issaquah, WA 98027-8654
Phone: 206-467-5157

Disabled Sports USA Northwest/Bellingham
110 Grand AVE
Bellingham, WA 98225
Phone: 360-676-0134
Email: dsusanw@dsusa.org
Web Site: www.dsusa.org/regions/nwreg/dsusanw

Mt. Baker Ski Area
1019 Iowa Street
Bellingham, WA 98226
Phone: 360-734-6771
Email: snow@mtbakerskiarea.com
Web Site: www.mtbakerskiarea.com

Ski Bluewood
P.O. Box 88
Dayton, WA 99328
Phone: 509-382-4725
Email: Info@bluewood.com
Web Site: WWW.Bluewood.com

Ski For All
1621 114th Avenue SE, Suite 132
Bellevue, WA 98004
Phone: 425-462-0978
Email: info@skiforall.org

Snoqualmie Pass
P.O. Box 1068
Snoqualmie Pass, WA 98068
Phone: 425-434-7669
Phone: 206-236-7277
Email: thesummit.sl@boothcreek.com
Web Site: www.summit-at-snoqualmie.com

Spokane Park & Recreation
808 W. Spokane Falls Blvd.
Spokane, WA 99201
Phone: 509-625-6245
Email: abusch@spokanecity.org
Web Site: www.spokanecity.org/parks

WEST VIRGINIA

Adaptive Sports at Snowshoe
Snowshoe Mountain
P.O. Box 10
Snowshoe, WV 26209
Phone: 304-572-6708
Email: dbegg@snowshoemtn.com
Web Site: www.zyworld.com/adaptive/Home.htm

Canaan Valley Resort & Conference Center
HC70, Box 330
Davis, WV 26260
Phone: 800-622-4121
Phone: 304-866-4121
Web Site: www.canaanresort.com

Snowshoe Adaptive Skiing/Challenged Athletes of WV
#1 Silver Creek Parkway
Snowshoe, WV 26209
Phone: 304-572-6708
Email: dbegg@snowshoemtn.com
Web Site: www.zyworld.com/adaptive/Home.htm
Web Site: www.snowshoemtn.com

Winterplace Ski Resort
P.O. Box 1
Flat Top, WV 25841
Phone 800 607-7669
Email: winterplace@winterplace.com
Web Site: www.winterplace.com

WISCONSIN

Blind Outdoor Leisure Development (Southeastern Wisconsin Lions)
1764 Blackhawk Trail
Waukesha, WI 53186-6905
Phone: 414-548-9114, President
1623 South 58th Street
West Allis, WI 53214
Phone: 414-328-0719 or 414-785-1188, Public Relations Director

Midstate Independent Living Center
P.O. Box 369
Rhinelander, WI 54501
Phone: 715-369-5040
Email: milc@newnorth.net
Web Site: www.indhwy.org

North Country Independent Living Center
P.O. Box 1245
Superior, WI 54880
Phone: 715-682-5676
Web Site: www.indhwy.org

SouthEastern Wisconsin Adaptive Ski Program (SEWASP)
W162 N11685 Park Avenue
Germantown, WI 53022
Phone: 262-502-4290, David Henderson
Email: info@sewasp.org
Web Site: www.sewasp.org

Trollhaugen
2232 100th Avenue
Dresser, WI 54009
Phone: 715-755-2955
Web Site: www.courage.org
(See Courage Center in Minneapolis, Minnesota)

WYOMING

Jackson Hole Mountain Resort
Box 290
3395 McCollister Drive
Teton Village, WY 83025
Phone: 307-733-2292
Phone: 888-DEEP-SNO
Email: olson@jacksonhole.com
Web Site: www.jacksonhole.com

Hogadon Ski Area
Alpine Adaptive Ski Program
1800 East K Street
Casper, WY 82601
Phone: 307-235-8499

Appendix H
Adaptive Equipment Suppliers

The following companies develop, manufacture, or distribute adaptive ski equipment.

Peter Axelson
Beneficial Designs
1617 Water Street, Suite B
Minden, NV 89423-4311
Phone: 775-783-8822
Email: mail@beneficialdesigns.com
Web Site: www.beneficialdesigns.com
Design and development of adaptive equipment for sit-down skiers.

Chris Devlin-Young
39 Alden Drive
Campton, NH 03223
Phone: 603-726-0098
Trench Digger 5000 (TD5000) mono-board

Paul Speight
Sports 'n Spokes
Enabling Technology
2225 S. Platte River Dr., W.
Denver, CO 80223
Phone: 303-922-0605
Email: info@spokesnmotion.com
Web Site: www.spokesnmotion.com
Manufacturer and distributor of Mono-skis, Unique Bi-skis, Superlite Outriggers, and Accessories. Videos on adaptive ski equipment and skiing techniques.

Evaluation P.E.P., Inc.
792 Lucien-Leclerc
Joliette, Québec, Canada J6E 3Z1
Phone: 450-760-9611

Email: evalpep@evaluation-pep.qc.ca
Web Site: www.evaluation-pet.qc.ca/anglais
Isoski Mono-ski, Bi-ski, Outriggers

Flex-Foot, Inc.
27412-A Laguna Hills
Aliso Viejo, CA, 92656
Phone: 800-233-6263
Phone: 949-362-3883
Email: information@flexfoot.com
Web Site: www.flexfoot.com
Designs and markets innovative lower limb prosthetic devices for amputees of all ages and activity levels.

Bill Grove
Grove Innovations
120 W. Church Street
Centre Hall, PA 16828
Phone: 814-364-2677
Email: tom@sitski.com
Web Site: www.sitski.com/grove.html
Mono-ski

Freedom Factory
Rt 5 Box 50734
Winnsboro, TX 75494
Phone: 903- 629-3945
Email: freefact@peoplescom.net
Web Site: sites.netscape.net/latvialynn/homepage
Revolution Pro Comp and Mogul Master V3 Mono-skis, Twin Ski, Mogul Master Two, Snow Slider Snow Walker

Mountain Man
720 Front Street
Bozeman, MT 59715
Phone: 406-587-0310
Sit-skis and Bi-skis

New Halls Wheels
P.O. Box 380784
Cambridge, MA 02238
Phone: 617-628-7955
Email: newhalls@tiac.net
Web Site: www.newhalls.com
Beast and Mt. Extreme Mono-skis

Next Step Orthotics and Prosthetics
9 Cedarwood Drive
Bedford, NH 03110
Phone: 603-668-3831
Web Site: www.NextstepOandP.com
Outriggers and Sports Prostheses

Obermeyer
Phone: 800-525-4203
Email: customerserv@obermeyer.com
Web Site: www.obermeyer.com
Mono-specific clothes

Praschberger
A-6341 Ebbs, Kleinfeld 8b
Germany
Phone: +43 (0) 5373/42570-0
Email: praschbergen@rolltechnik.com
Web Site: www.praschberger.com
Mono-ski

RadVentures
20755 SW 238th Place
Sherwood, OR 97140
Phone: 503-628-2895
Email: radyetti@aol.com
Web Site: www.radventures-yetti.com
Yetti Mono-skis, outriggers, ski legs and accessories

Reliable Racing Supply

643 Upper Glen St.
Queensbury, NY 12804
Phone: 518-793-5677
Email: customerservice@reliableracing.com
Web Site: www.reliable racing.com
Blind, Deaf, Vision-impaired Skier/Guide Bibs

Ski-Eze, Inc.
4401 Devonshire
Lansing, MI 48910
Phone: 517-882-4608
Email: skieze@gateway.net
Web Site: www.skieze.com
Ski Bras/Ski Handles

Strange Research & Development
PO Box 2247
Banff, Alberta, Canada TOL OCO
Phone: 403-762-5003
Email: strange@telusplanet.net
Web Site: www.sitski.com/strange3.htm
F1 Sit Ski

Appendix I
Resources

ABLEDATA
8630 Fenton Street, Suite 930
Silver Spring, MD 20910.
Phone: 800-227-0216
Email: abledata@macroint.com
Web Site: www.abledata.com
Provides information on assistive technology and rehabilitation equipment.

The American Blind Skiing Foundation
227 E. North Ave.
Elmhurst, IL 60126
Email: ABSF@bigfoot.com
Web Site: www.absf.org

Challenged Athletes Foundation
2148-B Jimmy Durante Blvd.
Del Mar, CA 92014
Phone: 858-793-9293
Email: execdir@challengedathletes.org
Web Site: www.challengedathletes.org
Assists and promotes physically disabled athletes in competitive pursuits.

Disabled Sports USA (DS/USA)
451 Hungerford Drive Suite 100
Rockville, MD 20850
Phone: 301-217-0960
Email: dsusa@dsusa.org
Web Site: www.dsusa.org

Extreme Adaptive Sports, Inc.
504 Brett Place
South Plainfield, NJ 07080
Phone: 908-313-5590
Email: eas@sitski.com

Web Site: www.sitski.com
Adaptive skiing and other extreme adaptive sports interactive resource
containing links to adaptive ski programs, equipment reviews, and a place
to voice your thoughts.

Kaleidoscope Sports & Entertainment, LLC.
136 Madison Avenue 8th Floor
New York, NY 10016
Phone: 212-779-6600
Email: bmadsen@nastar.com, Bill Madson, Director of Operations
Web Site: www.Nastar.com
Offers recreational NASTAR races around the country. Web Site includes
registration information and race standings.

National Ski Areas Association (NSAA)
133 S. Van Gordon Street, Suite 300
Lakewood, CO 80228
Phone: 303-987-1111
Email: nsaa@nsaa.org
Web Site: www.nsaa.org
Trade association for ski area owners and operators. NSAA represents 332
alpine resorts that account for more than 90 percent of the
skier/snowboarder visits nationwide. The organization also represents 436
supplier members who provide equipment, goods and services to the
mountain resort industry.

Sit Down Sports
11121 Forest Dr.
Anchorage, AK 99516
Phone: 907-349-9447
Email: lasher@micronet.net
Web Site: sitdownsports.com
Sit Down Sports is a community supported web resource for the disabled
athlete with information on sporting products, events, instruction,
associations, and photo galleries.

Ski TAM
PO Box 12700

Denver, CO 80212
Phone: 303-797-9507
Email: info@skitam.com
Web Site: www.skitam.com
An organization of the cable and telecommunications organization sponsoring annual benefit events to support the USDST.

U.S. Ski and Snowboard Association (USSA)
Box 100
1500 Kearns Blvd.
Park City, UT 84060
Phone: 435-649-9090
Email: special2@ussa.org
Web Site: www.usskiteam.com
The national governing body for Olympic skiing and snowboarding, provides information specifically on disabled ski classification, a roster and profiles of current team members.

U.S. Association of Blind Athletes (USABA)
33 North Institute Street
Colorado Springs, CO 80903
Phone: 719-630-0422
Web Site: www.usaba.org

World T.E.A.M. Sports
2108 South Blvd. Suite 101
Charlotte, NC 28203
Phone: 704-370-6070
Email: info@worldteamsports.org
Web Site: www.worldteamsports.org
Organizes and hosts sporting events with a special focus on athletes with disabilities.

Appendix J
Suggestions for Further Reading

Articles

Krag, Martin H MD, Messner, Duane G. MD. *Skiing by the Physically Handicapped* Clinics in Sports Medicine Vol. 1, No. 2, July, 1982. Department of Orthopaedics and Rehabilitation, University of Vermont College of Medicine, Given Building, Burlington, VT 05045

Books

May, Mike, ed. *Blind Alpine Skiing and Racing.* 5th ed. Talent, Oregon: Discovery Blind International, 1994.

O'Leary, Hal, ed. *Bold Tracks: Skiing for the Disabled.* 3rd ed. Boulder, Colorado: Johnson Books, 1994.

Sword, David. *Challenge Conditions.* Mount Hood, Oregon, 1988.

Wilson, Mike. *Right on the Edge of Crazy*: On Tour With the U.S. Downhill Ski Team. New York: Times Books, 1993.

Publications

Ability Magazine 1001 W. 17th Street, Costa Mesa, CA 92627
Phone: 949-854-8700 Email: subscriptions@abilitymagazine.com Web site: www.abilitymagazine.com
Magazine for the disability community. Discounted subscription rate offered through the web site.

Active Living, PO Box 237, Grimsby, Ontario L3M 4G3 Canada
Phone: 905-309-1639 Email: activelive@aol.com Web Site: www.cripworld.com/themall/activeliving.shtml
Focuses on how to improve health, fitness and mobility, where to enjoy accessible leisure and travel and what to look for in a new therapeutic, recreational or sporting activity.

Challenge Magazine, 451 Ungerford Drive, Suite 100, Rockville, MD 20850 Phone: 301-217-0960 Email: dsusa@dsusa.org Web Site: www.dsusa.org Publication of Disabled Sports USA.

Exceptional Parent Magazine, 555 Kinderkamack Road, Oradell, NJ 07649-1517
Phone: 201-634-6550 Web Site: www.eparent.com
Provides information, support, ideas, encouragement, and outreach for parents and families of children with disabilities and the professionals who work with them.

InMotion, Amputee Coalition of America, 900 E. Hill Avenue, Suite 285, Knoxville, TN 37915-2568
Phone: 865:254-8772 Web Site: www.amputee-coalition.org
Bi-monthly publication of the Amputee Coalition of America.

New Mobility, PO Box 220, Horsham, PA 19044
Phone: 215-675-9133 ext. 108 Email Ginal@jvleonard.com Web Site: www.newmobility.com
Web Site provides links to disability-related web sites and product information.

Palaestra: Challenge Publications, Ltd., PO Box 508, Macomb, IL 61455
Phone: 309-833-1902 Email: challpub@macomb.com. Web Site: www.palaestra.com
Forum of Sport, Physical Education & Recreation for Those With Disabilities. Published in cooperation with the United States Olympic Committee's Committee on Sports for the Disabled.

Paraplegia News, 2111 E. Highland Ave., Suite 180, Phoenix, AŻ 85016
Phone: 888-888-2201 X19 for subscriptions or 602-224-0500
Email: pvapub@aol.com
Web Site: www.pn-magazine.com
Magazine published by the Paralyzed Veterans of American. Includes articles of general interest as well as sports and recreation.

Ragged Edge Magazine, PO Box 145, Louisville, KY 40201

Web Site: www.ragged-edge-mag.com

Ski Racing Magazine, PO Box 1125, Waitsfield, VT 05673-1125
Phone: 802-496-7700 Email: sracing@skiracing.com Web Site: www.skiracing.com.
Magazine and web site cover able-bodied and disabled ski racing.
Sports 'n Spokes, the Magazine for Wheelchair Sports and Recreation. 2111 E. Highland Avenue, Suite 180, Phoenix, AZ 85016
Phone: 888-888-2201 x 19 for subscriptions, 602-224-0500 Email: snsmagaz@aol.com Web Site: www.sportsnspokes.com
Covers the latest in competitive wheelchair sports and recreational opportunities.

We Magazine, 495 Broadway, 6th Floor, New York, NY 10012
Phone: 800-963-2426 or 212-941-9584 Email: editors@wemagazine.com
Web Site: www.wemedia.com
Lifestyle magazine for people with disabilities.

Appendix K
Becoming Involved

Whether you are disabled or able-bodied, ski or prefer to watch sports from the comfort of your easy chair, many avenues exist for getting involved with adaptive skiing.

To learn to ski or improve your skills, contact your local ski area to see if they offer lessons for people with disabilities, or call one of the programs listed in Appendix G. When you contact them, be sure to ask about fees, schedules, and reservation policies as these vary widely between programs. You should also ask if the programs provide adaptive equipment and inquire about the experience and training of their ski instructors. The Professional Ski Instructors Association of America (PSIA) offers certified training programs specifically designed for teaching skiers with disabilities. PSIA-certified instructors must pass a rigorous set of tests both on-and-off the slopes before becoming certified. Adaptive ski programs also provide trained volunteers to assist disabled skiers.

When you're first learning to ski, properly fitted equipment can make a big difference in how quickly you pick up the sport. Lower-limb prostheses can be adapted to accommodate the natural forward-flexed ski position, and a good suspension system will provide extra stability on the slopes. If you have an SCI, make sure the seat of the mono- or bi-ski is adjusted correctly for your level of disability and provides enough stability and support.

Adaptive ski programs generally offer discounted prices for people with disabilities. Some programs also offer scholarships to those with financial constraints. For example, Jiminy Peak in Hancock, Massachusetts, where right arm amputee Adam Fromma began his skiing career, offers a $20 adaptive lift ticket, free equipment rental, and a free 3-hour lesson. Courage Duluth Alpine Ski Program in Minnesota, where gold medalist Monte Meier began skiing offers a $75 10-week lesson package on Tuesdays and Thursdays at Spirit Mountain. Waterville Valley in New Hampshire, which sponsored the race camp that began amputee skier Jason Lalla's road to the USDST offers group and private lessons any day of the season. Lesson prices range from $35 to $45, and include a lift ticket, adaptive ski equipment and instruction. Maine Handicapped Skiing's lessons at Sunday River are all free.

If ski racing appeals to you, at least three ski areas now offer specialized adaptive ski racing programs. The largest of these is the National Sports Center for the Disabled in Winter Park, Colorado, but the National Ability Center in Park City, Utah and the New England Disabled Ski Team at Loon in New Hampshire, also offer racing programs. Ski camps like the one offered by USDST mono-skiers Sarah Will and Chris Waddell in Vail, Colorado also help prepare skiers for competition. While some racers encourage learning through disabled ski race programs and camps, several USDST members raced on local able-bodied teams before being named to the national Team. Racing against able-bodied skiers can offer a different level of competition and increases the awareness of able-bodied skiers toward the athletic abilities of disabled ski racers.

If you are new to ski racing, it's best to first try a local NASTAR course to see if racing appeals to you. Each year DS/USA, listed in Appendix I, sponsors level 1 and level 2 regional races around the country. While level 1 races are designed to give beginning racers more experience, level 2 races allow you to compete against more experienced racers, often including USDST members. When the Team is in attendance, Team coaches are always present looking for new talent.

If you're an able-bodied skier interested in becoming involved with adaptive skiing, contact your local adaptive ski program or any of the programs listed in Appendix G regarding volunteer opportunities. Training programs vary from a weekend workshop to six-week trainings every weekend and usually begin in the fall. Volunteers learn about different disabilities, adaptive equipment and teaching techniques. Many adaptive programs also provide ski clinics throughout the year which volunteers are encouraged to attend to improve their skills and expand their knowledge base. In addition to honing your own skiing skills and meeting both able-bodied and disabled skiers, you'll receive free lift tickets and/or a season's pass and may receive other bonuses such as discounts on food, services, and merchandise at local ski shops. Most programs encourage volunteers to contact them early in the fall but some, including Winter Park's NSCD, send out applications as early as July. While not a requirement, many programs encourage volunteers to receive PSIA training and certification and some offer scholarships to offset some of the expenses.

Tahoe Adaptive Ski program in California has an on-going volunteer enrollment process throughout the year. However, they recommend contacting them about volunteering by October. Beginning volunteers receive a two-day introductory training and then may attend morning and half-day clinics throughout the season. Volunteers are required to participate four days during a season, although more time is appreciated. Based on the number of hours donated to the ski school, volunteers earn points toward lift tickets and other items.

Bromley Mountain in Vermont offers a volunteer training program on weekends throughout the season beginning in mid-November featuring in-house and guest trainers. Currently Bromley requires about twenty days a year from volunteers, though this is under review. Volunteers receive two lift tickets per day of training, teaching or assisting, including the day worked. Season's passes are given to qualifying volunteers in subsequent years.

The White Mountain Adaptive Ski School at Loon Mountain offers a mandatory orientation each October for everyone interested in volunteering. Each volunteer must pass a skiing tryout session then attend six-weeks of coaching. Their first year, volunteers receive a season's pass to Loon Mountain Resort and in subsequent years also earn a voucher for someone else to ski for each full day of coaching.

At the Adaptive Sports Center of Crested Butte in Colorado, first-time volunteers must attend an orientation then participate in a minimum of six clinics, including one on disability etiquette and another on general disability information. To earn a season's pass, volunteers must participate one and a half days per week, or 120 hours during the season. Non-pass volunteers receive a day pass for every two full days contributed.

The C.W. Hog adaptive ski program in Idaho provides volunteers with in-house training, which includes watching several videos on adaptive skiing and attending a two-day workshop on the mountain. The program prefers volunteers teach at least six lessons per season, but they encourage any volunteer to attend the training and help whenever they can, even if it's just a day or two per year.

At the National Ability Center in Park City, Utah beginning volunteers attend one two-to-four hour training session for the activity they are interested in where they are introduced to the program and the basic skills required. While there are no minimum time requirements, volunteers are asked to contribute as much as they can. Volunteers can earn a one-day lift pass for each day worked if they volunteer one day a week for the full five-week session and are invited to attend an end-of-the season party where they receive a small gift.

The NSCD in Winter Park, Colorado relies on approximately 1000 volunteers to assist its full-time staff of fifty. New volunteer applications are sent out each July with orientation held in October. Volunteers attend a four-to-six one-day per week training program and receive either complimentary tickets (for a five-day per season commitment) or a season's pass (for a ten-day per year commitment) to Winter Park. Volunteers may attend additional clinics throughout the ski season.

Even if you don't ski, you can support disabled skiing through your financial contribution by sponsoring an athlete or donating to any of several organizations that provide funds for disabled athletes and ski programs. Adaptive ski programs, which are funded in whole or in part by private donations, fundraisers, grants, and foundations, welcome contributions of any amount to enable them to offer affordable lift tickets, lessons, and equipment. Disabled ski racers find it difficult to receive financial assistance from major sponsors and are often in the position to borrow from family or obtain private funding to meet their yearly expenses which can range from $2,500 to over $10,000.

Contact the adaptive ski program of your choice to offer your financial support or equipment donation. To sponsor a member of the USDST, contact USSA at the address listed in Appendix I. By purchasing this book, you have already contributed to funding a USDST member. Another way to support disabled skiers is to make a donation to the Challenged Athletes Foundation (CAF), also listed in the appendix. CAF provides individual grants to athletes with a disability who are in need of funding for training, equipment, or travel expenses to major competitions. Since it's inception in 1994, the organization has raised almost $1,900,000 and assisted over 525 athletes with grant requests from around the world. Ninety percent of the funds go directly to assist disabled athletes, including many members of the USDST, and to an endowment fund. CAF's primary fundraiser is the San Diego Triathlon Challenge, which attracts elite athletes, challenged athletes, and celebrities from the US, Canada, and Mexico.

Another way to show your support for disabled ski racing is to attend regional and national races. Contact a nearby adaptive ski program to find out what races will be held in your area, or contact DS/USA for a calendar of sponsored races. While regional and national races spotlight both

USDST members and developing athletes, the World Cup, World Championships, and Paralympics attract the best disabled ski racers from around the world. Contact USSA for a listing of upcoming race dates and locations.

USDST members all agree they'd like to see more people show up at racing events in the United States. When competing in international races abroad, they notice spectators filling the stands and lining the slopes, sometimes up to five people deep at Paralympic games. Having that level of enthusiasm from spectators adds to the thrill and fulfillment of racing.

According to Dan Kosick, the best way to understand what disabled ski racing is all about is to watch athletes compete. "You can't really explain to a person who has never seen an elite athlete compete in the sport they do best," he says. "When they see it, you can tell they get it because they're like, 'No way! I thought you were fast, but that was *really* fast.' They just don't understand that we can not just do the same sport, but we can actually be very competitive with able-bodied people."

Jason Lalla, who has appeared in Warren Miller's extreme skiing films, agrees. "It's not disabled by any means. I basically let the skiing do the talking. I haven't met one person who's not impressed, from the able-bodied team down to the general population. It's just that people don't expect it to be at that high a level. And it is. It's all that and more."

Monte Meier gets the same response when people watch him ski. "It's a real eye-opening experience for people to see what people with disabilities are actually doing," he says. "You can explain it, but a picture is worth a thousand words. Everyone I've talked to who has seen it says, 'Oh my God, That's so amazing. I can't believe it.' I think it gets the public a little more aware of where we're at in this sport. We're not just a little weekend warrior group just having fun out there. This is a full-time round-the-calendar thing for us. I think if people see it, they actually get a chance to realize that it is pretty awesome."

Whatever way you choose to support the sport—financially, through your own participation, attending racing events, or telling your friends and neighbors about the exciting recreational and competitive opportunities available—you'll be contributing to the future of disabled skiing and helping disabled skiers reap the many benefits of alpine skiing.

Afterward
Parting Advice

No matter what your current level of skiing or what alpine dreams you aspire to, heeding some sound advice will make your experience on skis more rewarding. The main reason to take up skiing is for pure pleasure. For some, this means going out to the local area on weekends and swooshing down the mountain with friends and family. For others, it may mean years of training, hard work, and dedication both on and off the slopes to become one of the world's best ski racers. To become part of the Disabled Team, you've got to be serious about it. If you learn from the best, you can quite possibly be the best someday. But regardless of what level of skier you become, you will benefit from being out in the fresh air, exercising, learning new skills, and meeting new people.

For any level of skiing, the first thing to keep in mind is getting comfortable equipment. As amputee ski racer Dan Kosick learned when he spent money from his first big fundraiser, before you buy anything, think about your present level of skiing and future aspirations. A recreational skier will need different apparel and gear than a racer. In his excitement to get everything he thought he'd need, Dan bought a heavy ski jacket not realizing ski racers wear specially designed racing suits. And while everyone's heard of certain brand-name equipment, that doesn't mean it's right for you. Before buying, ask other disabled skiers what they're using, rent equipment, or try out different adaptive equipment available at your local ski area.

As much as possible, see that the equipment is adjusted and fitted for your specific level and type of disability. When mono-skier Muffy Davis first attempted adaptive skiing, her hometown ski area bought her a mono-ski—a generous gift worth $2,500. But since her instructors had no experience fitting a mono-ski, or teaching a disabled skier, Muffy gave up in frustration. Only when she hooked up with a knowledgeable instructor did she discover the true joy of mono-skiing.

Greg Mannino also recommends getting good equipment if you're serious about racing. Greg learned first hand that if you don't, it will show. He competed during the 1999-2000 season on poor equipment with even poorer results. When he finally borrowed some good skis for the Nationals, he beat everyone, "hands down." If you get good equipment, good guidance, and good coaching, you can win those Paralympic golds if that's what you want to do.

Sandy Dukat says that in addition to good ski equipment, amputees need to be sure to get a good prosthesis, especially a well-fitted socket. "I don't care if you have a top notch knee or foot, it won't matter," she says. "You need someone who's going to be able to build to fit your body." Finding a prosthetist who's willing to work with you to get the best fit is also important. Sandy's prosthetist at Hanger Prosthetics in Chicago is willing to build her another prosthesis if she experiences any problems. Nowadays, many prosthetists have experience with the latest lightweight prosthetic components and can make adjustments to your existing prosthesis or can build a custom-designed ski leg.

Before committing to the idea of ski racing, make sure you like it. Racing isn't for everyone. You need to love competition and be willing to put in long hours training, both on and off the slopes. After finding a local program to help you learn, or re-learn, to ski, if your aspirations include ski racing, first try a local NASTAR course. If you like that, hook up with a program that will allow you to ski frequently. Some adaptive ski programs run only one or two days per week, or for just a few weeks out of the season. But consistent training, both on and off the slopes is the key to becoming one of the best. As mono-skier Chris Waddell says, skiing is about miles and consistency—being able to make a turn consistently well so that you're not spending all your time recovering instead of picking up speed. Sarah Will believes that free skiing is one of the most important foundations for ski racing. She thinks it's a misconception that doing more gates improves racing skills. You need to feel the ski that you're on and that usually comes from free skiing, not running gates. In addition to developing strength, endurance, and technical skills, Sarah adds that it's important that skiers always work within their own comfort level.

While many USDST members spent a least some time training at the National Sports Center for the Disabled competition program at Winter Park, the largest disabled ski competition program in the country, others trained with Park City, the New England Ski Team, or other smaller programs. Still others trained with able-bodied teams. Training with able-bodied and disabled teams each have their unique benefits. Skiing with a disabled team gives you the opportunity to learn from others with the same or similar challenges as yours. When training with an able-bodied team, even though there's no one like you, they're generally better skiers.

Carl Burnett learned to race in the able-bodied program at Gould Academy before becoming involved with a disabled racing. He benefitted from the tougher courses and sometimes-longer hours of training and participated in the able-bodied races happening every weekend.

Chris Waddell continued to ski as a member of the Middlebury College team after he broke his back, becoming team captain his senior year before moving to Vail, Colorado to continue his training. Greg Mannino says that just getting in a good race program, either able-bodied or disabled, is key to becoming a successful ski racer and in his opinion, most of the able-bodied coaches across American now are savvy about disabled skiing.

Jason Lalla, who moved to Vail to train with the Team as soon as he set his goal of making the USDST, recommends going straight to the source. By doing that, Jason was able to see how he compared with the Team members. And he got to see what Team members were doing, not only on the racecourse, but also preparation-wise. Plus, he adds, he met great people who are "pretty fun." The problem with some of the smaller races, he says, is that they don't draw the same number of competitors, and that the U.S. Team doesn't attend all of them. And getting seen by Team coaches is an important step in being selected.

If you're the parent of a young child with a disability, you may or may not need to encourage them to become physically active. Many children adjust quickly to having a disability—even faster than a teen or adult. Parents can expose children to different sporting activities like skiing, but the most important thing is to just be supportive of whatever they want to do. After all, as Carl says, the job of a five-year-old is just to have fun. But if a child is going through a stage of not wanting to do anything and doesn't appear to be moving past it, Carl recommends offering a little bit of "tough love"—don't always help the child with things they can do for themselves.

Growing up in a small town in New York State, Dan Kosick felt somewhat sheltered and unaware of the numerous sports opportunities available to people with disabilities. He recommends talking to as many people as you can to learn what is available and how to get involved. He's found that unlike some of the able-bodied elite athletes who can seem unapproachable, elite disabled ski racers are more than willing to help out. "If they can't answer a question," he says, "they usually know someone who can." Dan admits he still goes to people for help and finds the longer he's on the Team, the more people turn to him for advice, giving him an opportunity to give back to others.

Jason agrees, recommending other disabled skiers not be shy about meeting people. While he's heard that some people think the Team members are unapproachable and tend to stay amongst themselves, the truth of the matter is that many of the Team members are together 150 to 200 days a year so a lot of them become best friends. But Jason's own experience of asking Team members if he could join them for lunch or dinner before he made the Team was that everyone was completely open which helped Jason learn what he needed.

While all the athletes admit winning medals is exciting, especially at international races like the Paralympics, World Cups, and World Championships, most focus on skiing their best, not on winning the gold. "Looking for the gold gives you too much pressure," says Monte Meier, whose career highlights include a gold medal in slalom at the 1998 Paralympics and a silver in giant slalom the same year. He feels focusing on the gold takes away from good skiing. If you go out there and do the best you can, the results will follow.

Muffy learned the hard way not to focus on medals. After winning three gold medals at her first international competition, she fell in the same three events two weeks later when competing at the 1998 Paralympics. Muffy partly blames the icy conditions for her falls, but realizes she also put too much pressure on herself to win. When she let go of all her expectations and told herself in the slalom she just wanted to finish two clean runs, she ended up winning the bronze.

As you train, remember that becoming a member of the USDST is not easy. In fact, blind skier Andy Parr says it's probably one of the hardest things he's done in his life. To succeed, you have to be a hard-working person, willing to ski fast, and love what you're doing. And, Andy says, don't give up. If you really want to do it, just keep going.

Chris Devlin-Young's biggest advice is "Try, try, try." Falling is part of learning to ski. You just need to get back up again. And Chris, who's competed in extreme snowboarding championships and synchronized skiing in addition to both mono- and stand-up skiing, adds that there's a brave new world out there. Many more options exist than when he started and many more people now have knowledge about those options. Give it a whirl. You've got nothing to lose except maybe a dry pair of pants.